PAVLOVA

FAVORITE RECIPES FROM

LA MERINGAIE

PARIS

Illustrations:

Emma Tissier

Writing and editorial coordination: Marie Vendittelli
Graphic design and art work: Florence Cailly
Translation from French: Carmella Abramowitz Moreau
and Ansley Evans

Copyright ©2017, Éditions de La Martinière, an imprint
of La Martinière Groupe for the original and English translation.
For the last edition: ©2017, Éditions de La Martinière, an imprint
of Groupe EDLM for the original and English translation.

ISBN: 978-1-4197-4370-2

Engraving: APS Chromostyle
Printed and bound in Printer Portuguesa
10 9 8 7 6 5 4 3 2

Abrams books are available at special discounts when
purchased in quantity for premiums and promotions as well
as fundraising or educational use. Special editions can
also be created to specification. For details, contact
specialsales@abramsbooks.com or the address below.

ABRAMS
The Art of Books

195 Broadway
New York, NY 10007
abramsbooks.com

PAVLOVA

FAVORITE RECIPES FROM

LA MERINGAIE

PARIS

MARIE STOCLET BARDON

with the collaboration of Charlotte Sindou-Faurie

Photography: Rina Nurra
Food styling: Sarah Vasseghi

Contents

PREFACE

I met Marie for the first time in 2007. Thus began a wonderful friendship and an exciting enterprise that culminated recently in a pastry shop, which after three years is considered one of the stars of the artisanal pastry-making scene in Paris. It is called La Meringaie.

During a conversation with Marie and her husband Benoît in 2014, they asked me what the word "meringue" conjured up for me.

My reply came in a flash: meringue is synonymous with good memories, festivities, and special treats. The mention of "meringue" instantly evokes simplicity and lightness.

More importantly, meringue plays an essential role in many pastry classics in France and elsewhere. Just think of the frozen vacherin; individual meringues flavored with chocolate, hazelnuts, almonds, or fresh fruit; and, of course, the pavlova.

Yet to me, a meringue is above all a small confection that takes me back to my childhood. Meringue comes in many guises—it can be plump, thin, fluted, smooth, pure white, caramelized, plain, or flavored—but sadly, it has been all too often forgotten over the last few decades by pastry chefs in France. The time had come to return this traditional recipe to its pedestal in the French pastry canon.

La Meringaie took up the challenge, devising an ethereal meringue to re-invent the classic pavlova—a nest for airy, unsweetened whipped cream with refreshing flavorings like citrus zest and fresh herbs and a colorful array of fresh fruits and berries.

La Meringaie's pavlovas are sheer delight for both the taste buds and the eyes, and they make for a luxurious treat for children and adults alike.

Their creations are spectacular: delectable, colorful pavlovas made with seasonal fruits at their peak, the finest chocolates, fresh whipping cream, almonds from Provence, hazelnuts from Piedmont—nothing but the most meticulously sourced ingredients.

As you can see, the adventure has only just begun for this crisp white cloud that simply melts in your mouth. La Meringaie will give you a new vision of meringue such as you could never have imagined.

GILLES MARCHAL

A MATCH MADE IN HEAVEN

There is no single "meringue": the past few centuries have seen the creation of Italian meringue, French meringue, and Swiss meringue, thanks to the method invented by Gasparini from Switzerland; it may have been popularized at the court of Louis XV by his Polish wife. Hypotheses about the invention of this voluptuous confection abound.

Let's take a closer look at how meringues came into being. It would appear that the dessert known as "snow" was first served in the sixteenth century. Then someone thought of adding sugar to the egg whites and cooking them very gently, a technique that seems to have led, in 1720, to the creation of a cake in the small town of Meiringen, in the Duchy of Saxe-Coburg Gotha, by a Swiss pastry chef named Gasparini. Some theories hold that this "meringue" was already served with whipped cream.

Later, Marie-Antoinette shared her love for the combination of whipped cream and meringue at the Court of Versailles. In fact, she was so enamored of this dessert that she would even whip the cream herself, and was known to don a dairymaid's outfit—true to Versailles trends of the time— to perform the task.

Antonin Carême, a renowned early nineteenth century chef and one of the founders of French grande cuisine, gave a new dimension to meringues by shaping them into rings and stacking them to make sculptural marvels. With the development of piping bags and whisks, the shapes of meringues evolved.

Closer to our time, in the 1920s, Anna Pavlova, the Russian prima ballerina, inspired a dessert during her tour of Australia and New Zealand. Both countries lay claim to the invention of the eponymous sweet. But no matter where it originated, the stunning pavlova had come into being, uniting the lightest whipped cream with a glossy meringue, a tribute to the celebrated dancer's tutu, with its frilly skirt and satiny bodice. With a meringue base that is crisp on the outside and delectably soft inside, a luscious layer of whipped cream, and endless combinations of fresh fruit, the pavlova is irresistible. One century later, it is popularly served at Christmas in both Australia and New Zealand.

The pavlovas we bring you in this book are variations on this stunning dessert, with our recipes based on the seasonality of fruits and flavors.

As a bonus, and to render homage to the delicious meringue that is the base of every pavlova, we have invited a number of renowned pastry chefs to contribute recipes inspired by this delicious sweet. We are sure you'll find their recipes as original as they are mouthwatering. Please join us as we explore the delights of this enchanting dessert. *Bon appetit*

THE EQUIPMENT

YOU'LL NEED TO MAKE OUR RECIPES

Fouet: **whisk**
Culs-de-poule: **round-bottomed mixing bowls**
Balance: **digital kitchen scale**
Couteaux: **knives**
Maryse: **flexible spatula**
Corne: **bowl scraper**
Batteur: **electric mixer**
Poche à douilles: **pastry bag**
Douilles: **piping tips**
Planche: **chopping board**

balance

culs-de-poule

fouet

couteaux

maryse

corne

planche

batteur

poche à douilles

douilles

TECHNIQUES:
STEP-BY-STEP

PREPARING
AND PIPING MERINGUE

SERVES 6 TO 8

FOR THE MERINGUE

5 LARGE EGG WHITES (5 OZ./150 G)
AT ROOM TEMPERATURE

1 CUP PLUS 1 TBSP. (7½ OZ./215 G) SUGAR

1½ TBSP. (15 G) CORNSTARCH

1 TSP. WHITE WINE VINEGAR

YOUR CHOICE OF SEASONINGS: A PINCH OF CINNAMON,
THE SEEDS FROM 1 VANILLA BEAN, ETC.

EQUIPMENT

TO MAKE THE MERINGUE: A WHISK
A STAND MIXER FITTED WITH A WHISK ATTACHMENT

TO PIPE THE MERINGUE: A DISPOSABLE PASTRY BAG
ICING TIPS OF VARIOUS SHAPES WITH ⅓- AND ⅜-INCH
(9- AND 10-MM) DIAMETERS

A BOWL SCRAPER OR FLEXIBLE SPATULA

PREPARING MERINGUE

1. Weigh your ingredients into small bowls. Precision is essential—the proportions in meringue are an exact science.

2. Pour the egg whites into the bowl of the stand mixer.

3. Add the sugar.

4. Then add the cornstarch.

5. Whisk to blend.

6. Begin beating at medium–high speed.

7. Continue for 10 minutes, until the whites hold firm, glossy peaks. Add the vinegar and beat for 1 additional minute.

8. If you are using seasonings, add them now. Beat for a few seconds, until just combined.

9. The meringue has the right texture for piping when it holds very firm peaks and does not flop over when the whisk is lifted.

PLAIN TIP

SAINT-HONORÉ
TIP

OPEN STAR
TIP

TECHNIQUES STEP-BY-STEP

DECIDE ON THE SHAPE YOU WILL BE PIPING OUT TO MAKE THE MERINGUE BASE (FLOWER, NEST, OR SWIRL) AND SELECT THE APPROPRIATE TIP(S).

PIPING AND BAKING MERINGUE

1. Preheat the oven to 210°F (100°C). Trim the tip of a pastry bag at about 1¼ inches (3 cm) from the bottom.

2. Open the bag and fold about one-third of the top downward to create a wide cuff.

3. Hold the bag under the cuff with one hand. Use your other hand to insert the tip into the bag and guide it down toward the hole.

4. Push the tip snugly into the hole—the bag should cover part of the tip.

5. Using a bowl scraper (or flexible spatula) scoop up a small amount of meringue mixture.

6. With the help of the hand under the cuff, transfer the meringue mixture into the bag.

7. Repeat the last two steps until the bag is half-full.

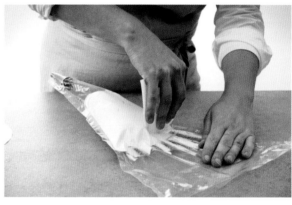

8. Lay the bag flat and, using the bowl scraper, push the meringue down toward the bottom of the bag, removing any air bubbles.

9. Once you have pushed the meringue all the way down, twist the bag tightly. Grip the bag in the palm of one hand at the twist and use your other hand to help guide your movements.

10. For a flower-shaped base, use two pastry bags, one fitted with an open star tip and the other with a plain tip, each tip measuring ⅓ and ⅜ inch (9 and 10 mm) in diameter. For your template, cut out a parchment paper circle slightly larger than a La Meringaie pavlova (10 inches/25 cm). With the bag fitted with the star tip, start piping out a spiral from the center.

11. Continue spiraling outward.

12. Stop piping when you have filled about three-quarters of the template.

13. Using the pastry bag with the plain tip, pipe out equal-size mounds around the edge of the circle. They should not overlap; be sure not to pipe right to the edges of the paper–meringue expands when baked.

14. Continue until you have completed the circle and formed a flower shape. You should end up with 11 to 12 mounds.

15. Bake the meringue for 1¾ hours, until crisp outside and slightly soft inside. Remove from the oven and let cool completely on the baking sheet.

PIPING OUT OTHER SHAPES

To make a nest-shaped meringue base, use a ⅜-inch (10-mm) plain tip to make the central spiral. Instead of piping mounds around the circumference, pipe out a border that is 1 to 1½ inches (3 to 4 cm) high.

Swirled meringue bases—the kind we use at La Meringaie—are the prettiest shape, but they are also by far the most difficult to make. For a swirled base, pipe out the central spiral with a pastry bag fitted with a ⅓-inch (9 mm) open star tip. Then cut the tip of a disposable pastry bag into the shape of a large Saint Honoré tip. To make the swirly rim, pipe each swirl from the outside of the circle toward the inside to make 11 to 12 swirls. Follow the same baking instructions used for the preceding meringue bases. You can also, of course, make larger or smaller pavlovas by adjusting the ingredients and the size of the centers proportionally. You will want 7 to 8 swirls or mounds around a pavlova to serve four and 13 to 14 swirls or mounds around a pavlova to serve eight.

CUTTING FRUIT

HOW TO CUT STRAWBERRIES

1. Wash the strawberries, carefully pat them dry, and hull them to remove the leafy top and the pale flesh directly beneath it.

2. Cut each strawberry into halves lengthwise.

3. Depending on the size of the strawberries, cut each half into several angled slices.
Use this method to cut apples, pears, mangoes, and more. It makes for a most attractive topping.

SEGMENTING CITRUS FRUITS

1. With a long, thin-bladed knife (a fish filleting knife is ideal, if you have one), trim each end of the orange.

2. Stand the orange upright on one of the ends. Angle the knife at the top of the peel, and work downward carefully to remove the peel in several pieces, turning the orange as you work.

3. Trim off any remaining white pith.

4. The orange is now ready for the next step: cutting into sections (*suprêmes* in French).

5. Hold the orange in one hand over a bowl to catch the juice, and hold the knife in the other hand.

6. Insert the knife along the membrane on one side of the section, and then on the other side.

7. With the knife, transfer the section carefully to a separate bowl.

8. Continue until you have removed all of the sections and only the membranes remain.

9. Squeeze out any remaining juice.

10. Your sections are ready to be placed on the pavlova.

ASSEMBLING YOUR PAVLOVA

1. Spoon the whipped cream into the center of the meringue base.

2. With the back of the spoon, spread the whipped cream in an even layer. It should stand slightly higher than the border design.

3. Arrange the first type of fruit attractively over the entire surface of the whipped cream.

4. Insert the second type of fruit between the first. To create the effect of a bouquet of wild flowers, stand the angled slices of fruit pointing upward (strawberries, mangoes, apples, and so on).

5. Lastly, insert the third type of fruit.

6. As a final flourish, scatter the top with garnishes like herbs, chopped nuts, or chocolate flakes or shavings, according to the recipe.

7. And there you have it! Refrigerate the pavlova until you are ready to serve it.

MAKING GANACHE

DARK CHOCOLATE GANACHE FOR 1 MERINGAIE PAVLOVA TO SERVE 6

7 OZ. (200 G) DARK CHOCOLATE, (70% CACAO)
¾ CUP (200 ML) WHIPPING CREAM

EQUIPMENT

A LARGE HEAVY IN THE SAUCEPAN
A HEATPROOF MIXING BOWL, PREFERABLY ROUND-BOTTOMED
A WHISK

1. If you don't have chocolate disks, chop the chocolate roughly. Bring the cream to a simmer and pour it over the chocolate.

2. Wait for a couple of minutes for the chocolate to begin to melt.

3. Using the whisk, begin stirring, making small circles at the center.

4. Continue stirring in small circles.

5. The chocolate now begins to rise in the center and the mixture changes color.

6. Make wider circles with the whisk, brushing against the sides of the bowl.

7. Continue until the mixture is perfectly smooth.

8. Now, simply wait for the ganache to cool enough to be spread over the meringue base.

LA MERINGAIE'S
PAVLOVAS

PÉLAGIE

Lime-Infused Whipped Cream,
Raspberries, and Passion Fruit

SUMMER-FALL

SERVES 6

1 MERINGUE BASE (see pages 14 to 20)

FOR THE WHIPPED CREAM	FOR THE TOPPING
¾ CUP (200 ML) WHIPPING CREAM, WELL CHILLED	3 PASSION FRUIT
ZEST OF 1 LIME, PREFERABLY ORGANIC	4 OZ. (125 G) RASPBERRIES
3 TBSP. (40 G) MASCARPONE	ZEST OF ½ LIME, PREFERABLY ORGANIC

PREPARATION | A day ahead, make the meringue base. To make the whipped cream layer, heat half of the cream, and just before it comes to a boil, pour it over the lime zest in a small bowl. Let cool slightly, cover with plastic wrap, and chill.

The next day, strain the infused cream into a well-chilled, round-bottomed mixing bowl, pressing down well on the zest to draw out maximum flavor. Stir in the remaining cream and mascarpone.

Using an electric mixer, whisk the preparation until it is smooth and holds firm peaks. Refrigerate until you are ready to assemble the pavlova.

To make the topping, scoop the seeds and pulp out of the passion fruit.

ASSEMBLY | Spread the whipped cream mixture evenly over the meringue base.
Arrange the raspberries over the cream, then drizzle with the passion fruit seeds and pulp. Decorate with the lime zest and chill until serving.

OUR TIPS | If you'd like the passion fruit to have a little firmness, use your favorite brand of pectin, following directions on the package for 3½ oz. (100 g) of fruit. Whisk over low heat until the mixture thickens to a sticky consistency. Add the passion fruit and stir until the mixture begins to steam, but do not allow it to boil as this might spoil the taste. Transfer to a chilled bowl and refrigerate. Before using, stir the preparation well to ensure that it is well- blended and drizzle over the whipped cream and raspberries.

VARIATIONS ON A THEME | Throughout the year, it is easy to find varieties of fruit that pair well with lime. You could try sweet mangoes, tangy pineapple, or flavorful strawberries.

FÉLICITÉ

Cocoa Whipped Cream, Raspberries, and Pears

FALL

SERVES 6

1 MERINGUE BASE (see pages 14 to 20)

FOR THE WHIPPED CREAM	FOR THE TOPPING
3 TBSP. (20 G) UNSWEETENED COCOA POWDER	2 PEARS
¾ CUP (200 ML) WHIPPING CREAM, WELL CHILLED	JUICE OF 1 LEMON
1½ BSP. (20 G) SUGAR	4 OZ. (125 G) RASPBERRIES
	DARK CHOCOLATE SHAVINGS FOR DECORATING

PREPARATION | A day ahead, make the meringue base.
The next day, make the whipped cream layer: Combine the cocoa powder with the cream and sugar in a well-chilled, round-bottomed mixing bowl. Using an electric mixer, whisk the preparation until it is smooth and holds firm peaks. Refrigerate until you are ready to assemble the pavlova.
To make the topping, peel the pears and cut them into angled slices. Squeeze a little lemon juice over them to prevent browning.

ASSEMBLY | Spread the cream mixture evenly over the meringue base. Arrange the raspberries over the cream, then the pear slices, and scatter with chocolate shavings. Chill until serving.

OUR TIPS | Cream combined with cocoa powder whips up quickly, so to ensure that it remains smooth without turning grainy, do not over-whisk it.

VARIATIONS ON A THEME | Other fruits are particularly good with chocolate, too. Try subbing orange sections, apricots, or bananas for the pears.

DÉSIRÉE

Coconut Whipped Cream, Mango,
Kiwifruit, and Pomegranate

WINTER

SERVES 6

1 MERINGUE BASE (see pages 14 to 20)

FOR THE WHIPPED CREAM	**FOR THE TOPPING**
SCANT ½ CUP (100 ML) WHIPPING CREAM, WELL CHILLED	½ MANGO
SCANT ½ CUP (100 ML) COCONUT CREAM	2 RIPE KIWIFRUIT
3 TBSP. (40 G) MASCARPONE	¼ POMEGRANATE
	COCONUT FLAKES OR UNSWEETENED SHREDDED COCONUT (OPTIONAL)

PREPARATION | A day ahead, make the meringue base.
The next day, make the whipped cream layer: Place the whipping cream, coconut cream, and mascarpone in a well-chilled, round-bottomed mixing bowl. Using an electric mixer, whisk the preparation until it is smooth and holds firm peaks. Refrigerate until you are ready to assemble the pavlova.
To make the topping, peel the mango, cut it away from the pit, and cut it into angled slices. Peel the kiwifruit and slice them into quarter-rounds, then seed the pomegranate.

ASSEMBLY | Spread the cream mixture evenly over the meringue base. Arrange the mango over the cream, and place the kiwifruit slices between the mango slices. Dot with the pomegranate seeds. If you wish, sprinkle with coconut flakes or shredded coconut. Chill until serving.

VARIATIONS ON A THEME | You might want to add a small dash of rum to the cream, swap the kiwifruit and pomegranate for pineapple and passion fruit, and scatter the pavlova with lime zest. You've almost got a piña colada!

AUGUSTINE

Red Berry Tea-Infused Whipped Cream, Strawberries,
Raspberries, and Red Currants

SPRING-SUMMER

SERVES 6

1 MERINGUE BASE (see pages 14 to 20)

FOR THE WHIPPED CREAM	FOR THE TOPPING
¾ CUP (200 ML) WHIPPING CREAM, WELL CHILLED	4 OZ. (125 G) STRAWBERRIES
1 TBSP. (10 G) LOOSE-LEAF BLACK TEA WITH MIXED BERRIES	4 OZ. (125 G) RASPBERRIES
3 TBSP. (40 G) MASCARPONE	A FEW RED CURRANTS FOR DECORATING

PREPARATION | A day ahead, make the meringue base. To make the whipped cream layer, pour half of the cream over the tea. Cover with plastic wrap and chill.
The next day, strain the infused cream into a well-chilled, round-bottomed mixing bowl, removing all the tea leaves. Stir in the remaining cream and mascarpone. Using an electric mixer, whisk the preparation until it is smooth and holds firm peaks. Refrigerate until you are ready to assemble the pavlova.
To make the topping, wash, dry, and hull the strawberries and cut each one into two or three angled slices. Pick the red currants from the stems.

ASSEMBLY | Spread the cream mixture evenly over the meringue base. Arrange the raspberries over the cream, and then the strawberries and red currants. Chill until serving.

OUR TIPS | Making a cold infusion ensures that all the flavors of the fragile ingredients infused—teas, herbal teas, aromatic herbs, flowers, and so on—are preserved.

VARIATIONS ON A THEME | The wide range of loose-leaf teas available opens a world of possibilities for flavoring cream. Try other fruit-flavored teas, Earl Grey tea, or matcha tea. All of them are excellent with the assorted red berries in this recipe.

ZÉLIE

Orange Zest-Flavored Whipped Cream,
Oranges, Mango, and Passion Fruit

WINTER

SERVES 6

1 MERINGUE BASE (see pages 14 to 20)

FOR THE WHIPPED CREAM	FOR THE TOPPING
¾ CUP (200 ML) WHIPPING CREAM, WELL CHILLED	2 PASSION FRUIT
ZEST OF 1 ORANGE, PREFERABLY ORGANIC	1 MANGO
3 TBSP. (40 G) MASCARPONE	2 LARGE SEEDLESS ORANGES, SUCH AS NAVEL OR VALENCIA

PREPARATION | A day ahead, make the meringue base. To make the whipped cream layer, heat half of the cream to just before boiling, then pour it over the orange zest in a small bowl. Let cool slightly, cover with plastic wrap, and chill.
The next day, strain the infused cream into a well-chilled, round-bottomed mixing bowl, ensuring no zest remains. Stir in the remaining cream and mascarpone.
Using an electric mixer, whisk the preparation until it is smooth and holds firm peaks. Chill until you are ready to assemble the pavlova.
To make the topping, scoop out the seeds and pulp from the passion fruit.
Peel the mango, remove the pit, and cut the flesh into angled slices. Peel the oranges and separate them into sections (see page 22).

ASSEMBLY | Spread the cream mixture evenly over the meringue base. Arrange the orange sections over the cream, followed by the mango and passion fruit. Chill until serving.

OUR TIPS | To ensure that the cream whips up well, it must be well chilled. If possible, place it in the freezer for 15 minutes before whisking it. The mixing bowl should also be nice and cold.

VARIATIONS ON A THEME | If you're a citrus lover, you might want to replace the mango and passion fruit with blood oranges and grapefruit.

HONORINE

*Timur Pepper-Infused Whipped Cream,
Litchis, Grapefruit, and Raspberries*

WINTER

SERVES 6

1 MERINGUE BASE (see pages 14 to 20)

FOR THE WHIPPED CREAM	FOR THE TOPPING
¾ CUP (200 ML) WHIPPING CREAM, WELL CHILLED	1 GRAPEFRUIT
ABOUT 10 TIMUR PEPPERCORNS, CRUSHED	ABOUT 10 LITCHIS
3 TBSP. (40 G) MASCARPONE	4 OZ. (125 G) RASPBERRIES

PREPARATION | A day ahead, make the meringue base. To make the whipped cream layer, heat half of the cream. Just before it comes to a boil, pour it over the peppercorns in a small bowl. Let cool slightly, cover with plastic wrap, and chill.
The next day, strain the infused cream into a well-chilled, round-bottomed mixing bowl and stir in the remaining whipping cream and mascarpone. Using an electric mixer, whisk the preparation until it is smooth and holds firm peaks. Refrigerate until you are ready to assemble the pavlova.
To make the topping, separate the grapefruit into sections (see page 22). Peel the litchis and slice them.

ASSEMBLY | Spread the cream mixture evenly over the meringue base. Arrange the raspberries and grapefruit over the cream, followed by the litchis. Chill until serving.

OUR TIPS | From Nepal, the highly aromatic Timur peppercorns (also known as Timut peppercorns) impart slightly spicy citrus notes to the cream. If you can't find this particular variety, simply replace it with another peppercorn, such as Ganshu or Sichuan either green or red.

VARIATIONS ON A THEME | This recipe is an ode to tanginess. Should you prefer, you can play around with the fruits according to the seasons, combining several citrus fruits or, more generally, other fruits with a tart zing.

VIOLETTE

Violet-Scented Whipped Cream,
Figs, Blueberries, and Pears

SUMMER

SERVES 6

1 MERINGUE BASE (see pages 14 to 20)

FOR THE WHIPPED CREAM	FOR THE TOPPING
¾ CUP (200 ML) WHIPPING CREAM, WELL CHILLED	3 FIGS
1 DROP VIOLET FLAVORING	1 FIRM, RIPE PEAR
3 TBSP. (40 G) MASCARPONE	JUICE OF 1 LEMON
	4 OZ. (125 G) BLUEBERRIES
	A FEW TOASTED HAZELNUTS, COARSELY CHOPPED

PREPARATION | A day ahead, make the meringue base.
The next day, make the whipped cream layer: In a well-chilled, round-bottomed mixing bowl, combine the whipping cream, violet flavoring, and mascarpone. Using an electric mixer, whisk the preparation until it is smooth and holds firm peaks. Refrigerate until you are ready to assemble the pavlova.
To make the topping, cut the figs into quarters and the pear into angled slices. Drizzle the pear slices lightly with the lemon juice.

ASSEMBLY | Spread the cream mixture evenly over the meringue base. Arrange the figs and pears over the cream. Dot the blueberries between the other fruits. Sprinkle with the chopped hazelnuts and chill until serving.

VARIATIONS ON A THEME | Floral flavors with whipped cream and fruit make for a delightful threesome. Do try other natural flavorings—rose, lavender, jasmine, poppy, and so on—which are just as delicious with summer fruit, such as apricots and white and yellow peaches and nectarines. The choice is yours!

VALENTINE

*Rose-Scented Whipped Cream,
Raspberries, and Litchis*

WINTER

SERVES 6

1 MERINGUE BASE (see pages 14 to 20)

FOR THE WHIPPED CREAM
¾ CUP (200 ML) WHIPPING CREAM,
WELL CHILLED
SCANT ½ CUP (100 ML) ROSE WATER
3 TBSP. (40 G) MASCARPONE
1 DROP PINK NATURAL FOOD
COLORING (OPTIONAL)

FOR THE TOPPING
ABOUT 10 LITCHIS
4 OZ. (125 G) RASPBERRIES

PREPARATION | A day ahead, make the meringue base.
The next day, make the whipped cream layer: In a well-chilled, round-bottomed
mixing bowl, combine the cream, rose water, and mascarpone. Add the coloring
if using. With an electric mixer, whisk the preparation until it is smooth and holds firm
peaks. Refrigerate until you are ready to assemble the pavlova.
To make the topping, peel and slice the litchis.

ASSEMBLY | Spread the cream mixture evenly over the meringue base. Arrange
the raspberries over the cream. Insert the litchi slices between the raspberries and chill
until serving.

OUR TIPS | To round out the floral notes in the cream, you could add a little honey
to the mixture. Serve this pavlova along with a glass of champagne or muscat wine,
both of which are marvelous with litchis.

VARIATIONS ON A THEME | Rose flavoring goes well with other flavorings and
ingredients, such as cardamom, vanilla, pistachio, and citrus zest. Should you wish
to try one of them, simply infuse it in half of the cream a day ahead (see page 31) and
the next day, strain the infused cream if necessary and combine it with the remaining
cream, mascarpone, and rose water. Then follow the instructions above to whisk
the preparation.

EUPHRASIE

*Orange Blossom-Scented Whipped Cream,
Oranges, Bananas, and Dates*

WINTER

SERVES 6

1 MERINGUE BASE (see pages 14 to 20)

FOR THE WHIPPED CREAM
¾ CUP (200 ML) WHIPPING CREAM,
WELL CHILLED

1 TBSP. (15 ML) ORANGE BLOSSOM
WATER

3 TBSP. (40 G) MASCARPONE

FOR THE TOPPING
3 LARGE SEEDLESS ORANGES,
SUCH AS NAVEL OR VALENCIA

1 NOT-TOO-RIPE BANANA

JUICE OF 1 LEMON

A FEW MEDJOOL DATES

½ OZ. (15 G) PINE NUTS
(ABOUT 2 TBSP.)

PREPARATION | A day ahead, make the meringue base.

The next day, make the whipped cream layer: In a well-chilled, round-bottomed mixing bowl, combine the cream, orange blossom water, and mascarpone. With an electric mixer, whisk the preparation until it is smooth and holds firm peaks. Refrigerate until you are ready to assemble the pavlova.

To make the topping, separate the orange into sections (see page 22). Peel the banana, slice it into rounds, and drizzle with the lemon juice to prevent browning. Pit the dates and slice them lengthwise. Lightly toast the pine nuts.

TO ASSEMBLE | Spread the cream mixture evenly over the meringue base. Arrange the orange sections over the cream, followed by the banana. Place the pieces of date between the sections. Sprinkle with the pine nuts and chill until serving.

OUR TIPS | Serve this dessert with mint tea or a spicy tea, such as chai.

VARIATIONS ON A THEME | Orange blossom water is a flavor for all seasons. To transform this recipe into a summery dessert, swap the oranges and bananas for strawberries, rhubarb, peaches, or cherries.

EULALIE

Ginger Whipped Cream,
Rhubarb, and Strawberries

SPRING

SERVES 6

1 MERINGUE BASE (see pages 14 to 20)

FOR THE WHIPPED CREAM	FOR THE TOPPING
¾ OZ. (20 G) FRESH GINGER (ABOUT 3 INCHES)	3 STALKS RHUBARB
¾ CUP (200 ML) WHIPPING CREAM, WELL CHILLED	1¼ CUPS (8 OZ./250 G) SUGAR
3 TBSP. (40 G) MASCARPONE	SEEDS OF 1 VANILLA BEAN (OPTIONAL)
	8 OZ. (250 G) STRAWBERRIES

PREPARATION | A day ahead, make the meringue base. To make the whipped cream layer, peel the ginger and dice it finely, then crush the dice with the back of a knife. Heat half of the cream together with the diced ginger and remove from the heat just before it comes to a boil. Let cool slightly, cover with plastic wrap, and chill.

To make the topping, finely slice the rhubarb. Combine the sugar with 1 cup (250 ml) of water in a saucepan, adding the vanilla seeds if you wish. Bring to a boil and carefully pour over the sliced rhubarb. Cover with plastic wrap flush with the surface, let cool slightly, and chill for at least 12 hours or overnight, ensuring the pieces remain firm (see Our tips).

The next day, strain the infused cream into a well-chilled, round-bottomed mixing bowl. Stir in the remaining cream and mascarpone. Using an electric mixer, whisk the preparation until it is smooth and holds firm peaks. Refrigerate until you are ready to assemble the pavlova. Wash, dry, and hull the strawberries and cut each into two or three angled slices. Drain the rhubarb slices.

ASSEMBLY | Spread the cream mixture evenly over the meringue base. Arrange the strawberries over the cream and dot the rhubarb slices, which should still be firm, between the strawberries. Chill until serving.

OUR TIPS | Rhubarb happens to be one of our favorite fruits, but it's one that is difficult to work with. When it's raw, it's quite tart, but when it's cooked, it softens to mush. Macerating it overnight in a syrup maintains just the right amount of firmness while fully developing the flavors of the fruit. This technique can also be used for certain other fruits such as slightly hard pears and apples.

VARIATIONS ON A THEME | For a slightly sweeter version of this recipe, make vanilla whipped cream, following the recipe on page 62.

BÉRÉNICE

Milk Chocolate-Passion Fruit Ganache,
Nectarines, Raspberries, and Mango

SUMMER

SERVES 6

1 MERINGUE BASE (see pages 14 to 20)

FOR THE WHIPPED GANACHE

5 OZ. (150 G) MILK CHOCOLATE
(40% CACAO), CHOPPED

SCANT ½ CUP (100 ML) WHIPPING
CREAM TO HEAT

SCANT ½ CUP (100 ML) WHIPPING
CREAM, WELL CHILLED

2¼ OZ. (70 G) STRAINED PASSION
FRUIT PULP

FOR THE TOPPING

½ MANGO

2 LARGE NECTARINES

4 OZ. (125 G) RASPBERRIES

PREPARATION | A day ahead, make the meringue base. To make the whipped ganache, place the chocolate in a round-bottomed mixing bowl. Heat the cream to a simmer and pour it over the chocolate. Wait 2 minutes, then make the ganache (see page 26). Stir in the passion fruit pulp and then the chilled cream. Cover with plastic wrap and chill.
The next day, use an electric mixer to whisk the ganache until it is light and airy and return to the refrigerator.
To make the topping, peel and pit the mango and cut the flesh into angled slices. Leave the nectarines unpeeled and cut them into angled slices.

ASSEMBLY | Spread the whipped ganache evenly over the meringue base. Arrange the raspberries, mango, and nectarines over the ganache. Chill until serving.

VARIATIONS ON A THEME | Instead of nectarines, try different varieties of peeled peaches. Those with more tang pair well with the whipped milk chocolate ganache in this recipe.

ANATOLIE

White Chocolate and Pistachio Ganache,
Strawberries, and Pears

SUMMER

SERVES 6

1 MERINGUE BASE (see pages 14 to 20)

FOR THE WHIPPED GANACHE	FOR THE TOPPING
5 OZ. (150 G) WHITE CHOCOLATE, CHOPPED	2 PEARS
¾ CUP (200 ML) WHIPPING CREAM	JUICE OF 1 LEMON
2 OZ. (50 G) PISTACHIO PASTE	4 OZ. (125 G) STRAWBERRIES
	1 TBSP. CHOPPED PISTACHIOS

PREPARATION | A day ahead, make the meringue base. To make the whipped ganache, place the chocolate in a round-bottomed mixing bowl. Heat the cream to a simmer with the pistachio paste, mixing well. It is advisable to use an immersion blender to combine the two ingredients thoroughly. Pour the mixture over the white chocolate and wait for 2 minutes, then make the ganache (see page 26). Let cool slightly, cover with plastic wrap, and chill.
The next day, whisk the ganache with an electric mixer to ensure that it is light and airy and return to the refrigerator.
To make the topping, peel the pears and cut them into angled slices. Squeeze over a little lemon juice to prevent browning. Wash, dry, and hull the strawberries and cut each into two or three angled slices.

ASSEMBLY | Spread the whipped ganache evenly over the meringue base. Arrange the strawberries and pears over the ganache. Sprinkle with the chopped pistachios and chill until serving.

OUR TIPS | Pistachio paste tends to stick, so when we combine it with cream, we use an immersion blender for utmost smoothness.

VARIATIONS ON A THEME | Pistachio-flavored ganache is excellent with other red berries, such as raspberries, cherries, and red currants.

SOPHIE

*Chestnut Cream, Whipped Cream,
Oranges, Candied Orange Peel,
and Candied Chestnuts*

WINTER

SERVES 6

1 MERINGUE BASE (see pages 14 to 20)

FOR THE WHIPPED CREAM	FOR THE TOPPING
¾ CUP (200 ML) WHIPPING CREAM, WELL CHILLED	2 LARGE SEEDLESS ORANGES, SUCH AS NAVEL OR VALENCIA
2 TBSP. (30 G) MASCARPONE	A FEW CANDIED CHESTNUTS (*MARRONS GLACÉS*)
1 TBSP. (20 G) CHESTNUT CREAM, CHILLED, FOR THE BASE (*CRÈME DE MARRONS*, SEE OUR TIPS)	A LITTLE CANDIED ORANGE PEEL
	CHOCOLATE SHAVINGS

PREPARATION | A day ahead, make the meringue base, piping it into either a round or rectangular shape (a rectangle should be about 4 inches wide and 10 to 12 inches long/10 cm by 25 to 30 cm).

The next day, prepare the whipped cream layer. Place the cream and mascarpone in a well-chilled, round-bottomed mixing bowl. Using an electric mixer, whisk the preparation until it is smooth and holds firm peaks. Refrigerate until you are ready to assemble the pavlova.

To make the topping, separate the oranges into sections (see page 22), and break the candied chestnuts into small pieces.

ASSEMBLY | Spread the chestnut spread over the meringue base and then spread the whipped cream evenly over that. Arrange the orange sections, candied orange peel, and candied chestnut pieces over the whipped cream, and scatter with chocolate shavings. Chill until serving.

OUR TIPS | It's best to chill the chestnut spread before assembling the pavlova. This ensures that you retain the original texture of the meringue. You can use a pastry bag to pipe it out instead of simply spreading it.

VARIATIONS ON A THEME | This recipe, which includes ingredients typically used for desserts for the festive season in France—candied chestnuts and orange peel—is a fine example of how fresh oranges can offset the more indulgent candied components. Make the dessert even more scrumptious by drizzling chocolate sauce over each portion!

MARCELINE

Honey Whipped Cream, Blackberries,
Raspberries, Red Currants, and Blueberries

SUMMER

SERVES 6

1 MERINGUE BASE (see pages 14 to 20)

FOR THE WHIPPED CREAM	FOR THE TOPPING
¾ CUP (200 ML) WHIPPING CREAM, WELL CHILLED	2 OZ. (60 G) RASPBERRIES
3 TBSP. HONEY	2 OZ. (60 G) BLACKBERRIES
3 TBSP. (40 G) MASCARPONE	2 OZ. (60 G) BLUEBERRIES
	A FEW RED CURRANTS

PREPARATION | A day ahead, make the meringue base. To make the whipped cream layer, heat half of the cream and pour it over the honey in a small bowl. Mix well to combine, let cool slightly, cover with plastic wrap, and chill. This hot infusion, prepared ahead of time, releases the full aroma of the honey.

The next day, stir the remaining cream and mascarpone into the honey-cream infusion in a well-chilled, round-bottomed mixing bowl. Using an electric mixer, whisk the preparation until it is smooth and holds firm peaks. Refrigerate until you are ready to assemble the pavlova.

ASSEMBLY | Spread the cream mixture evenly over the meringue base. Arrange the raspberries, blackberries, and blueberries over the cream, and then the red currants. Chill until serving.

VARIATIONS ON A THEME | If you incorporate a little raspberry or red currant coulis into the cream mixture just before whisking it, your version of the recipe will have a more intense fruity taste as well as a little extra tang.

BERTILLE

*Dulcey Ganache, Bananas,
Raspberries, Mango, and Speculaas*

FALL

SERVES 6

1 MERINGUE BASE (see pages 14 to 20)

FOR THE WHIPPED GANACHE	FOR THE TOPPING
5 OZ. (150 G) BLOND DULCEY CHOCOLATE CHOPPED	2 BANANAS
¾ CUP (200 ML) WHIPPING CREAM	JUICE OF 1 LEMON
	½ MANGO
	2 OZ. (60 G) RASPBERRIES
	4 SPECULAAS COOKIES

PREPARATION | A day ahead, make the meringue base. To make the whipped ganache, place the chocolate in a round-bottomed mixing bowl. Heat the cream to a simmer and pour it over the chocolate. Wait 2 minutes, then make the ganache (see page 26). Let cool slightly, cover with plastic wrap, and chill.
The next day, whisk the ganache with an electric mixer to ensure that it is light and airy and return to the refrigerator.
To make the topping, cut the bananas into rounds and drizzle with a little lemon juice to prevent browning. Peel the half mango, remove the pit, and cut the flesh into angled slices.

ASSEMBLY | Spread the whipped ganache evenly over the meringue base. Arrange the raspberries and banana slices over the ganache. Crush the speculaas cookies and scatter them over the top. Chill until serving.

OUR TIPS | All of our recipes can be made in shot glasses. Should you wish to make this version, spoon the whipped ganache into a pastry bag so that you can easily pipe it into the base of each glass. Lightly crush the meringues, sprinkle them over the base layer, spread another layer of ganache over that, and top with the fruit pieces.

VARIATIONS ON A THEME | If you are a speculaas fan, crush a few cookies and incorporate them into the ganache.

ARTÉMISE

*Cinnamon Berry-Infused Whipped Cream,
Pineapple, Grapefruit, and Zante Currants*

WINTER

SERVES 6

1 MERINGUE BASE (see pages 14 to 20)

FOR THE WHIPPED CREAM	FOR THE TOPPING
¾ CUP (200 ML) WHIPPING CREAM, WELL CHILLED	1¼ CUPS (8 OZ./250 G) SUGAR
2 TBSP. (15 G) CINNAMON BERRIES (SEE OUR TIPS)	1 CINNAMON STICK OR THE SEEDS OF 1 VANILLA BEAN (OPTIONAL)
3 TBSP. (40 G) MASCARPONE	1 HANDFUL ZANTE CURRANTS
	1 GRAPEFRUIT
	⅓ PINEAPPLE
	1 HANDFUL TOASTED MACADAMIA NUTS

PREPARATION | A day ahead, make the meringue base. To make the whipped cream layer, heat half of the cream. Just before it comes to a boil, pour it over the cinnamon berries in a small bowl. Cool slightly, cover with plastic wrap, and chill.

To make the topping, combine the sugar with 1 cup (250 ml) of water in a saucepan, adding the cinnamon stick or vanilla seeds if you wish. Bring to a boil, remove from the heat, and pour over the currants in a bowl. Let soak for 12 hours or overnight.

The next day, strain the infused cream into a well-chilled, round-bottomed mixing bowl and stir in the remaining cream and mascarpone. Using an electric mixer, whisk the preparation until it is smooth and holds firm peaks. Refrigerate until you are ready to assemble the pavlova.

For the topping, drain the currants and separate the grapefruit into sections (see page 22). Peel and core the pineapple, remove any eyes, and cut the fruit into bite-size pieces.

ASSEMBLY | Spread the cream mixture evenly over the meringue base. Arrange the grapefruit and pineapple over the cream, followed by the currants and macadamia nuts. Chill until serving.

OUR TIPS | Cinnamon berries are the fruit of the Ceylon cinnamon tree, whose bark is used for the spice we commonly call "cinnamon." The berries add a more subtle cinnamon taste to the cream as well as mildly peppery notes.

VARIATIONS ON A THEME | Try replacing the fruits in this recipe with pears lightly poached in red wine and fresh or candied oranges and, *voilà*, you have the typical flavors of mulled wine!

DAPHNÉ

*Vanilla Whipped Cream,
Strawberries, and Bananas*

SPRING-SUMMER

SERVES 6

1 MERINGUE BASE (pages 14 to 20 and Our tips)

FOR THE WHIPPED CREAM

¾ CUP (200 ML) WHIPPING CREAM,
WELL CHILLED

1 VANILLA BEAN, SPLIT LENGTHWISE
AND SEEDS SCRAPED

3 TBSP. (40 G) MASCARPONE

FOR THE TOPPING

8 OZ. (250 G) STRAWBERRIES

2 BANANAS

JUICE OF 1 LEMON

SMALL CHOCOLATE FLAKES

PREPARATION | A day ahead, make the meringue base, piping out individual bases if you wish (see Our tips). To make the whipped cream layer, heat half of the cream with the vanilla bean and seeds. Just before the mixture comes to a boil, remove it from the heat and transfer it to a cold container. Let cool slightly, cover with plastic wrap, and chill.

The next day, remove the vanilla bean from the cream and pour it into a well-chilled, round-bottomed mixing bowl. Stir in the remaining cream and mascarpone. Using an electric mixer, whisk the preparation until it is smooth and holds firm peaks. Refrigerate until you are ready to assemble the pavlova.

To make the topping, wash, dry, and hull the strawberries and cut each into two or three angled slices. Slice the bananas into rounds and drizzle with a little lemon juice to prevent browning.

ASSEMBLY | Spread the cream mixture evenly over the meringue base, then arrange the strawberries over the cream, followed by the bananas. Sprinkle with the chocolate flakes and chill until serving.

OUR TIPS | To pipe out individual meringue bases, take inspiration from the step-by-step instructions on page 19—simply make a small mound in the center surrounded by mounds of the same size to form a flower shape.

VARIATIONS ON A THEME | To accentuate the deliciously retro appeal of this recipe with hints of banana split, drizzle warm dark chocolate syrup over each serving.

ANTOINETTE

Lemon-Basil Whipped Cream,
Melon, and Strawberries

SUMMER

SERVES 6

1 MERINGUE BASE (see pages 14 to 20)

FOR THE WHIPPED CREAM

¾ CUP (200 ML) WHIPPING CREAM, WELL CHILLED

10 LEAVES FRESH BASIL, CHOPPED

ZEST OF 1 LEMON, PREFERABLY ORGANIC

3 TBSP. (40 G) MASCARPONE

FOR THE TOPPING

¼ GREEN-FLESHED MELON, SUCH AS HONEYDEW OR GALIA

8 OZ. (250 G) STRAWBERRIES

PREPARATION | A day ahead, make the meringue base. To make the whipped cream layer, pour half of the cream over the basil and zest in a small bowl, cover with plastic wrap, and chill.

The next day, strain the infused cream into a well-chilled, round-bottomed mixing bowl, pressing down well on the basil and zest. Stir in the remaining cream and mascarpone. Using an electric mixer, whisk the preparation until it is smooth and holds firm peaks. Refrigerate until you are ready to assemble the pavlova.

To make the topping, remove the seeds and rind from the melon and cut the fruit into angled slices. Wash, dry, and hull the strawberries and cut each into two or three angled slices.

ASSEMBLY | Spread the cream mixture evenly over the meringue base, then arrange the melon over the cream, followed by the strawberries. Chill until serving.

VARIATIONS ON A THEME | Herbs are an infinite source of original ideas for flavoring whipped cream: try cilantro, mint, tarragon, dill—anything that suits your fancy! You can also try raspberries, plums, or citrus with the melon rather than strawberries.

ZEINAH

*Date Cream, Sesame Whipped Cream,
Raspberries, and Oranges*

SPRING

SERVES 6

1 MERINGUE BASE (see pages 14 to 20)

FOR THE DATE CREAM
3½ OZ. (100 G) FRESH DATES, PITTED
SCANT ½ CUP (100 ML)
WHIPPING CREAM
2 TBSP. SUGAR

FOR THE WHIPPED CREAM
¾ CUP (200 ML) WHIPPING CREAM,
WELL CHILLED
2 TBSP. (20 G) LIGHTLY TOASTED
SESAME SEEDS
3 TBSP. (40 G) MASCARPONE

FOR THE TOPPING
2 LARGE SEEDLESS ORANGES,
SUCH AS NAVEL OR VALENCIA
A FEW TOASTED WHOLE ALMONDS
4 OZ. (125 G) RASPBERRIES

PREPARATION | A day ahead, make the meringue base.
To make the date cream, combine the dates, cream, and sugar in a saucepan
and cook over low heat just until the fruit has softened, then puree the mixture
in a blender or food processor until smooth and chill.
To make the whipped cream layer, heat half of the cream with the sesame seeds.
Just before the mixture comes to a boil, remove it from the heat. Process with
a blender or food processor until combined, cover with plastic wrap, and chill.
The next day, strain the sesame-infused cream into a well-chilled, round-bottomed
mixing bowl and stir in the remaining cream and mascarpone. Using an electric mixer,
whisk the preparation until it is smooth and holds firm peaks. Refrigerate until you are
ready to assemble the pavlova.
To make the topping, separate the oranges into sections (see page 22) and roughly
chop the almonds.

ASSEMBLY | Spread the date cream evenly over the meringue base, followed
by the whipped cream. Arrange the orange sections and raspberries over the cream,
then decorate with the almonds. Chill until serving.

VARIATIONS ON A THEME | You could also flavor the whipped cream with orange
blossom water, which pairs brilliantly with date cream.

ANGÉLIQUE

*Dark Chocolate Ganache,
Strawberries, Cherries, and Blueberries*

SPRING-SUMMER

SERVES 6

1 MERINGUE BASE (see pages 14 to 20)

FOR THE WHIPPED GANACHE

5 OZ. (150 G) DARK CHOCOLATE
(70% CACAO), CHOPPED

¾ CUP (200 ML) WHIPPING CREAM
TO HEAT

⅔ CUP (150 ML) WHIPPING CREAM,
WELL CHILLED

FOR THE TOPPING

4 OZ. (125 G) STRAWBERRIES

1 HANDFUL CHERRIES

1 HANDFUL BLUEBERRIES

PREPARATION | A day ahead, make the meringue base. To make the whipped ganache, place the chocolate in a round-bottomed mixing bowl. Heat the cream to a simmer and pour it over the chocolate. Wait 2 minutes, then make the ganache (see page 26). Let cool slightly, cover with plastic wrap, and chill.
The next day, thin the ganache with the well-chilled whipping cream. Using an electric mixer, whisk the ganache until it is light and airy, taking care not to over beat (see Our tips). Return to the refrigerator.
To make the topping, wash, dry, and hull the strawberries and cut each into two or three angled slices, then halve and pit the cherries.

ASSEMBLY | Spread the whipped ganache evenly over the meringue base. Arrange the strawberries over the ganache, then the cherries and blueberries. Chill until serving.

OUR TIPS | A ganache is an emulsion. If you follow the step-by-step instructions on page 26, your ganache will be perfectly smooth. But be careful when beating—ganache whips up quickly! Watch it closely so that it does not turn grainy.

VARIATIONS ON A THEME | *To add complexity to the ganache, try infusing the cream with 1¼ teaspoons (2 g) of crushed Timur peppercorns, for instance, the day before (see page 40).*

ROSALIE

Rosemary Whipped Cream,
Apricots, Mango, and Melon

SUMMER

SERVES 6

1 MERINGUE BASE (see pages 14 to 20)

FOR THE WHIPPED CREAM
¾ CUP (200 ML) WHIPPING CREAM,
WELL CHILLED
3 SPRIGS ROSEMARY
3 TBSP. (40 G) MASCARPONE

FOR THE TOPPING
3 RIPE APRICOTS
½ MANGO
¼ MELON OF YOUR CHOOSING
A FEW SPRIGS ROSEMARY

PREPARATION | A day ahead, make the meringue base. To make the whipped cream layer, heat half of the cream. Just before it comes to a boil, pour it over the rosemary sprigs in a small bowl. Let cool slightly, cover with plastic wrap, and chill.
The next day, strain the infused cream into a well-chilled, round-bottomed mixing bowl and stir in the remaining cream and mascarpone. Using an electric mixer, whisk the preparation until it is smooth and holds firm peaks. Refrigerate until you are ready to assemble the pavlova.
To make the topping, remove the pits from the apricots, peel and pit the mango, and remove the rind and seeds from the melon. Cut the fruits into angled slices.

ASSEMBLY | Spread the cream mixture evenly over the meringue base and arrange the fruit slices on top. Decorate with the rosemary sprigs and chill until serving.

VARIATIONS ON A THEME | You could also add a little rosemary honey to the whipped cream for a sweeter touch.

PÉTRONILLE

Dill Whipped Cream, Cherries,
Pink Grapefruit, and Figs

SUMMER

SERVES 6

1 MERINGUE BASE (see pages 14 to 20)

FOR THE WHIPPED CREAM	FOR THE TOPPING
¾ CUP (200 ML) WHIPPING CREAM, WELL CHILLED	1 PINK GRAPEFRUIT
½ BUNCH DILL, CHOPPED	A FEW FIGS
3 TBSP. (40 G) MASCARPONE	2 OZ. (50 G) CHERRIES
	A FEW SPRIGS DILL (OPTIONAL)

PREPARATION | A day ahead, make the meringue base. To make the whipped cream layer, pour half of the cream over the dill in a small bowl, cover with plastic wrap, and chill.

The next day, strain the infused cream into a well-chilled, round-bottomed mixing bowl and stir in the remaining cream and mascarpone. Using an electric mixer, whisk the preparation until it is smooth and holds firm peaks. Refrigerate until you are ready to assemble the pavlova.

To make the topping, separate the grapefruit into sections (see page 22), then cut the figs into angled slices. Halve and pit the cherries, reserving one whole cherry with the stem on for decoration.

ASSEMBLY | Spread the cream mixture evenly over the meringue base. Arrange the grapefruit over the cream followed by the figs and cherries. Decorate with dill sprigs if you wish and chill until serving.

VARIATIONS ON A THEME | To play with the flavors and colors, you could try this recipe using only melon, combining different varieties. All melons work well with the anise notes of the dill.

CÉSARINE

*Maple Whipped Cream,
Apples, Grapes, and Pecans*

FALL

SERVES 6

1 MERINGUE BASE (see pages 14 to 20)

FOR THE WHIPPED CREAM
¾ CUP (200 ML) WHIPPING CREAM,
WELL CHILLED
2 TBSP. (30 ML) MAPLE SYRUP
3 TBSP. (40 G) MASCARPONE

FOR THE TOPPING
3 APPLES, SUCH AS JAZZ, FUJI,
OR ROYAL GALA, UNPEELED
JUICE OF 1 LEMON
1 BUNCH SEEDLESS RED GRAPES
1 HANDFUL TOASTED PECANS

PREPARATION | A day ahead, make the meringue base.
The next day, make the whipped cream layer: Combine the cream, maple syrup, and mascarpone in a well-chilled, round-bottomed mixing bowl. Using an electric mixer, whisk the preparation until it is smooth and holds firm peaks. Refrigerate until you are ready to assemble the pavlova.
To make the topping, cut the apples into angled slices and drizzle with a little lemon juice to prevent browning (see Our tips). Cut the grapes in half and roughly chop the pecans.

ASSEMBLY | Spread the cream mixture evenly over the meringue base. Pat the apple slices dry if necessary and arrange them over the cream, followed by the grapes. Decorate with the pecans and chill until serving.

OUR TIPS | If you want the apples to be tender, make a syrup by heating 1¼ cups (8 oz./250 g) of sugar to boiling with 1 cup (250 ml) of water, adding a split vanilla bean for flavor if you wish. Add the apple slices (no lemon juice necessary) and cook for a few minutes, until they reach the desired consistency. Remove from the syrup, let cool slightly, and refrigerate until you are ready to assemble the pavlova.

VARIATIONS ON A THEME | Maple syrup is of course a Canadian icon, and the country produces many delicious apple varieties, too. In this recipe, you could try combining two or three different types of apples with a range of colors, flavors, and textures.

PIMPRENELLE

Carambar® Whipped Cream, Strawberries, Apples, and Mini Marshmallows

SUMMER

SERVES 6

1 MERINGUE BASE (see pages 14 to 20)

FOR THE WHIPPED CREAM	FOR THE TOPPING
¾ CUP (200 ML) WHIPPING CREAM, WELL CHILLED	4 OZ. (125 G) STRAWBERRIES
15 CARAMBAR® CANDIES, OR 3½ OZ.	1 GRANNY SMITH APPLE, UNPEELED (SEE OUR TIPS)
3 TBSP. (40 G) MASCARPONE	¼ CUP MINIATURE MARSHMALLOWS (ABOUT 20)
(100 G) OTHER CARAMEL CANDIES	

PREPARATION | A day ahead, make the meringue base. To make the whipped cream layer, heat half of the cream with the Carambar® candies, stirring until they are fully melted. Let cool slightly, cover with plastic wrap, and chill.

The next day, pour the candy-cream mixture into a well-chilled, round-bottomed mixing bowl and stir in the remaining cream and mascarpone. Using an electric mixer, whisk the preparation until it is smooth and holds firm peaks. Refrigerate until you are ready to assemble the pavlova.

To make the topping, wash, dry, and hull the strawberries and cut them into angled slices, then cut the apple into angled slices, too.

ASSEMBLY | Spread the cream mixture evenly over the meringue base. Arrange the strawberries and apples over the cream, followed by the marshmallows. Chill until serving.

OUR TIPS | It is best to use tart apples like Granny Smiths in this recipe to round out the sweetness of the caramel.

VARIATIONS ON A THEME | Have fun with your kids! Many types of candy are perfect for flavoring whipped cream, such as fruit-flavored gummy candies, licorice, and so on.

URSULINE

Saffron Whipped Cream, Strawberries,
Raspberries, and Red Bell Pepper

SUMMER

SERVES 6

1 MERINGUE BASE (see pages 14 to 20)

FOR THE WHIPPED CREAM	FOR THE TOPPING
¾ CUP (200 ML) WHIPPING CREAM, WELL CHILLED	1 RED BELL PEPPER
30 SAFFRON THREADS	1 TBSP. SUGAR
3 TBSP. (40 G) MASCARPONE	4 OZ. (125 G) STRAWBERRIES
	2 OZ. (60 G) RASPBERRIES

PREPARATION | A day ahead, make the meringue base. To make the whipped cream layer, heat half of the cream. Just before it comes to a boil, pour it over the saffron threads in a small bowl. Let cool slightly, cover with plastic wrap, and chill.
To make the topping, preheat the oven to 250°F (120°C). Peel the bell pepper, cut it in half, and remove the white parts and seeds. Cut into strips and roast on a parchment-lined baking sheet for 2 hours. Puree the roasted pepper with the sugar to make a sweet coulis and refrigerate.
The next day, strain the saffron infused cream into a well chilled, round bottomed mixing bowl and stir in the remaining cream and mascarpone. Using an electric mixer, whisk the preparation until it is smooth and holds firm peaks. Refrigerate until you are ready to assemble the pavlova.
Wash, dry, and hull the strawberries and cut them into angled slices.

ASSEMBLY | Spread the cream mixture evenly over the meringue base. Arrange the strawberries over the cream, then dip the raspberries into the red bell pepper coulis and place them between the strawberry slices. If you like, drizzle a little coulis between the berries. Chill until serving.

OUR TIPS | If you are feeling bold, use roasted bell pepper strips instead of coulis between the berries.

VARIATIONS ON A THEME | Vegetables are another excellent source of inspiration for adding an original touch to your pavlovas. Fennel, for instance, with its anise notes, would be delicious with an anise-scented whipped cream and pears.

PHILOMÈNE

*Bitter Almond-Flavored Whipped Cream,
Peaches, Apricots, Blackberries, and Cherries*

SUMMER

SERVES 6

1 MERINGUE BASE (see pages 14 to 20)

FOR THE WHIPPED CREAM	FOR THE TOPPING
¾ CUP (200 ML) WHIPPING CREAM, WELL CHILLED	1 YELLOW PEACH
1 DROP BITTER ALMOND EXTRACT	2 APRICOTS
3 TBSP. (40 G) MASCARPONE	1 HANDFUL CHERRIES
	A FEW BLACKBERRIES
	EDIBLE FLOWERS (OPTIONAL)
	WHOLE ALMONDS (OPTIONAL)

PREPARATION | A day ahead, make the meringue base.

The next day, make the whipped cream layer: Combine the cream, almond extract, and mascarpone in a well-chilled, round-bottomed mixing bowl. Using an electric mixer, whisk the preparation until it is smooth and holds firm peaks. Refrigerate until you are ready to assemble the pavlova.

To make the topping, remove the pits from the peach and apricots and cut the fruit into bite-size pieces. Halve and pit the cherries and cut the blackberries in two.

ASSEMBLY | Spread the cream mixture evenly over the meringue base. Arrange the peaches and apricots over the cream, then the cherries and blackberries. If you like, decorate the pavlova with a few edible flowers and almonds.

VARIATIONS ON A THEME | To make this pavlova even more delectable, add a scant ¼ cup (20 g) of ground toasted almonds to the meringue just before it reaches the firm peak stage. If you add them any earlier, the meringue could turn liquid.

ROMY

*Popcorn-Infused Whipped Cream,
Strawberries, and Cherries*

SPRING-SUMMER

SERVES 6

1 MERINGUE BASE (see pages 14 to 20)

FOR THE WHIPPED CREAM
¾ CUP (200 ML) WHIPPING CREAM,
WELL CHILLED
SCANT 2 CUPS (20 G) POPCORN
(SEE OUR TIPS)
1 PINCH FINE SEA SALT
2½ TSP. (10 G) SUGAR
3 TBSP. (40 G) MASCARPONE

FOR THE TOPPING
1 HANDFUL CHERRIES
8 OZ. (250 G) STRAWBERRIES
CARAMEL POPCORN
FOR DECORATING

PREPARATION | A day ahead, make the meringue base. To make the whipped cream layer, heat the cream with the popcorn, salt, and sugar. Just before the cream comes to a boil, remove it from the heat, cover, and let infuse for 10 minutes. In a blender or food processor, process the cream mixture until combined, then strain and chill it. The next day, pour the infused cream into a well-chilled, round-bottomed mixing bowl and stir in the mascarpone. Using an electric mixer, whisk the preparation until it is smooth and holds firm peaks. Refrigerate until you are ready to assemble the pavlova.
To make the topping, halve and pit the cherries, then wash, dry, and hull the strawberries and cut them into angled slices.

ASSEMBLY | Spread the cream mixture evenly over the meringue base. Arrange the cherries and strawberries over the cream. Decorate with the caramel popcorn just before serving so that it stays crisp.

OUR TIPS | Making the popcorn yourself—either in the microwave or on the stovetop—will make this pavlova even better. Be sure to infuse the popcorn in the cream while the popped kernels are still warm.

VARIATIONS ON A THEME | The flavor of popcorn is excellent with berries, but you can improvise with what's in season. A combination of apples and pears with chocolate flakes would be a great choice in the fall.

AIMÉE

*Coffee Ganache, Pears,
and Sweet and Sour Cherries*

SUMMER OR WINTER

SERVES 6

1 MERINGUE BASE (see pages 14 to 20)

FOR THE WHIPPED GANACHE
5 OZ. (150 G) WHITE CHOCOLATE, CHOPPED
⅓ CUP (150 ML) WHIPPING CREAM
1 TSP. (5 G) COFFEE EXTRACT (SEE OUR TIPS)

FOR THE TOPPING
2 RIPE BUT FIRM PEARS
JUICE OF 1 LEMON
A FEW SWEET CHERRIES
ABOUT 10 SOUR CHERRIES
A FEW TOASTED HAZELNUTS

PREPARATION | A day ahead, make the meringue base. To make the whipped ganache, place the chocolate in a round-bottomed mixing bowl. Heat the cream to a simmer with the coffee extract, stirring until well blended. Pour the cream over the chocolate and wait 2 minutes, then make the ganache (see page 26). Let cool slightly, cover with plastic wrap, and chill.
The next day, use an electric mixer to whisk the ganache until it is light and airy and return to the refrigerator.
To make the topping, peel the pears, cut them into angled slices, and drizzle with a little lemon juice to prevent browning. Halve and pit the sweet and sour cherries and roughly chop the hazelnuts.

ASSEMBLY | Spread the whipped ganache evenly over the meringue base. Arrange the pears over the ganache, then the sweet and sour cherries and hazelnuts. Chill until serving.

OUR TIPS | You can make your own coffee extract by heating 1½ cups (350 ml) of water to boiling with ¾ cup (5 oz./150 g) of sugar. Let the syrup cool to 40°F (4°C), then stir in 1 cup (3½ oz./100 g) of ground coffee. Let infuse for 24 hours in the refrigerator.
The next day, heat the syrup to about 120°F (50°C) and strain it through extra-fine cheesecloth. Reheat the strained syrup to a simmer over low heat and cook, stirring frequently, until it has reduced by two-thirds—heating the syrup slowly prevents it from burning. It is best to use a mild roasted coffee with sweet notes so that the extract is not too bitter. We use the coffee grown using biodynamic farming methods in the Araku Valley in India.

VARIATIONS ON A THEME | Coffee pairs famously with chocolate, so this pavlova is absolutely scrumptious with warm chocolate syrup. If you take this route, you could use pears only. To make the chocolate syrup, follow the ganache recipe on page 26 and drizzle while still warm.

PHILIPPINE

Cardamom and Rose-Scented Whipped Cream, Apricots, Nectarines, and Cherries

SUMMER

SERVES 6

1 MERINGUE BASE (see pages 14 to 20)

FOR THE WHIPPED CREAM

¾ CUP (200 ML) WHIPPING CREAM, WELL CHILLED

1½ TSP. (4 G) GREEN CARDAMOM PODS

3 TBSP. (40 G) MASCARPONE

1 TBSP. ROSE WATER

FOR THE TOPPING

3 RIPE APRICOTS

1 OR 2 NECTARINES, DEPENDING ON THE SIZE

1 HANDFUL CHERRIES

1 HANDFUL CHOPPED PISTACHIOS

PREPARATION | A day ahead, make the meringue base. To make the whipped cream layer, heat half of the cream. Just before it comes to a boil, pour it over the cardamom pods in a small bowl. Let cool slightly, cover with plastic wrap, and chill. The next day, strain the infused cream into a well-chilled, round-bottomed mixing bowl and stir in the remaining cream, mascarpone, and rose water. Using an electric mixer, whisk the preparation until it is smooth and holds firm peaks. Refrigerate until you are ready to assemble the pavlova.

To make the topping, remove the pits from the apricots and nectarines and cut the fruit into angled slices. Halve and pit the cherries.

ASSEMBLY | Spread the cream mixture evenly over the meringue base. Arrange the apricots and nectarines over the cream, then the cherries. Sprinkle with the pistachios and chill until serving.

OUR TIPS | For an extra-sweet touch, drizzle a little honey over the pavlova just before serving.

VARIATIONS ON A THEME | You can replace the rose water with orange blossom water, which is equally outstanding with the fruits in this recipe.

OUR
MERINGUETTES

MERINGUETTES

Chocolate, Hazelnut, Almond, and Pistachio

MAKES ABOUT 100 MERINGUETTES

FOR THE MERINGUE	FOR THE TOPPINGS
5 LARGE EGG WHITES (5 OZ./150 G), AT ROOM TEMPERATURE	THIN CHOCOLATE FLAKES (ABOUT 1 OZ./25 G)
1 CUP PLUS 1 TBSP. (7½ OZ./215 G) SUPERFINE SUGAR	TOASTED SHREDDED COCONUT (PREFERABLY UNSWEETENED)
1½ TBSP. (15 G) CORNSTARCH	CHOPPED NUTS, SUCH AS HAZELNUTS, PISTACHIOS, ALMONDS, AND WALNUTS
1 TSP. WHITE WINE VINEGAR	DARK AND MILK CHOCOLATE, SHAVED

PREPARATION | To make the meringue, pour the egg whites into the bowl of a stand mixer with the sugar and cornstarch. Whisk at medium-high speed for about 8 minutes. The resulting meringue should be firm and glossy, so if necessary, increase the whisking time. Drizzle in the vinegar and whisk for 1 additional minute.
Preheat the oven to 210°F (100°C) and line two (or three, if necessary) baking sheets with parchment paper.

MERINGUETTES WITH CHOCOLATE FLAKES | Make sure that the chocolate flakes are small enough to be squeezed through the nozzle of the icing tip. Incorporate them evenly into the meringue mixture and scoop into a pastry bag fitted with a ⅜-inch (1-cm) plain tip (see page 17). Working rapidly, pipe out 1-inch (2.5-cm) diameter domes (see Our tips), leaving an inch or more between them—they will expand while baking. If you wish, sprinkle them with toasted shredded coconut, chopped nuts, or chocolate shavings. Bake for 1 hour, until crisp outside and slightly soft inside, let cool completely on the baking sheets, then store in an airtight container.

MERINGUETTES WITH NUTS | Pipe the plain meringue into domes of the same size and with the same space between them. Sprinkle with the chopped nuts and bake as above. Let cool completely on the baking sheets, then store in an airtight container.

OUR TIPS | Once the meringue mixture is ready, quickly stir in the additional ingredients and pipe out. If left too long, the meringue will become liquid and be difficult to bake. Stored correctly, these meringuettes will keep for 2 to 3 weeks.

VARIATIONS ON A THEME | Add a fun touch to these mini confections with a little natural food coloring stirred into the meringue mixture. If you stir it in very briefly rather than completely, you'll have pretty striations.

MOOKIES

MAKES ABOUT 10 MOOKIES

FOR THE MERINGUE
5 LARGE EGG WHITES (5 OZ./150 G), AT ROOM TEMPERATURE
1 CUP PLUS 1 TBSP. (7½ OZ./215 G) SUPERFINE SUGAR
1½ TBSP. (15 G) CORNSTARCH
1 TSP. WHITE WINE VINEGAR

FOR THE TOPPINGS
1 OZ. (25 G) FINE CHOCOLATE FLAKES, PLUS MORE FOR SPRINKLING
GRATED ZEST OF 1 LEMON, PREFERABLY ORGANIC, OR
1 TBSP. FRUIT POWDER (SUCH AS STRAWBERRY OR RASPBERRY)

7 OZ. (200 G) DARK CHOCOLATE, MINIMUM 70% CACAO OR
7 OZ. (200 G) MILK CHOCOLATE, MINIMUM 35% CACAO, OR HALF OF EACH
CHOPPED NUTS, SUCH AS HAZELNUTS, PISTACHIOS, ALMONDS, AND WALNUTS, OR SHREDDED COCONUT
FRESH RASPBERRIES (OPTIONAL)

PREPARATION | To make the meringue, pour the egg whites into the bowl of a stand mixer with the sugar and cornstarch. Whisk the egg whites at medium-high speed for about 8 minutes. The resulting meringue should be firm and glossy, so if necessary, increase the whisking time. Drizzle in the vinegar and whisk for 1 additional minute. Preheat the oven to 210°F (100°C) and line a baking sheet with parchment paper.

MOOKIES WITH CHOCOLATE FLAKES | Make sure that the chocolate flakes are small enough to be squeezed through the nozzle of the icing tip. Incorporate them evenly into the meringue mixture and scoop into a pastry bag fitted with a plain ⅜-inch (1-cm) tip (see page 17). Pipe out flower shapes (see page 18), leaving an inch or more between them—they will expand while baking. Sprinkle with more chocolate flakes and bake for 1 hour, until crisp outside, slightly soft inside, and easy to lift from the parchment paper. Let cool completely on the baking sheet and store in an airtight container.

FRUIT MOOKIES | Stir the lemon zest or fruit powder into the prepared meringue mixture. When it is evenly distributed, pipe out the mookies in flower shapes (see page 18), leaving an inch or more between them, as they expand while baking. Bake for 1 hour, until crisp to the touch, slightly soft inside, and easy to lift from the parchment paper. Let cool completely on the baking sheet and store in an airtight container.

CHOCOLATE-DIPPED MOOKIES | Make plain mookies following the piping and baking instructions above. When they are completely cool, melt the chocolate (dark or milk, or half of both) and carefully dip the top half of each mookie into it. Wait until all the excess has dripped off so that you have a neat line. Place on a baking sheet lined with parchment paper. If you wish, before the chocolate sets, sprinkle with chopped nuts or shredded coconut. You can also top the mookies with fresh raspberries. Refrigerate until set.

OUR TIPS | If you want the chocolate to have a lovely sheen, you can temper it beforehand. Chop two-thirds of the chocolate you have opted to use and set it to melt over a hot water bath. Meanwhile, finely chop the remaining third. When the melted chocolate is perfectly smooth, remove it from the heat and add the remaining chopped chocolate. Let it melt gently. When the mixture is smooth again, bring a little to your lips to test the temperature. It should be warm but not feel hot—you're aiming for a temperature of 88°F (31°C). If the chocolate firms up before you have finished topping the mookies, reheat it, ensuring that the temperature does not exceed 88°F (31°C).

VARIATIONS ON A THEME | While the chocolate topping is still soft, dot the mookies with fresh fruit, such as raspberries or orange sections.

MERINGUE LADYFINGERS

MAKES 40 TO 50 LADYFINGERS

FOR THE MERINGUE
5 LARGE EGG WHITES (5 OZ./150 G),
AT ROOM TEMPERATURE
1 CUP PLUS 1 TBSP. (7½ OZ./215 G)
SUPERFINE SUGAR
1½ TBSP. (15 G) CORNSTARCH
1 TSP. WHITE WINE VINEGAR

FOR DIPPING
7 OZ. (200 G) DARK CHOCOLATE,
MINIMUM 70% CACAO
OR 7 OZ. (200 G) MILK CHOCOLATE,
MINIMUM 35% CACAO, OR HALF
OF BOTH

CHOPPED NUTS, SUCH
AS HAZELNUTS, PISTACHIOS,
ALMONDS, AND WALNUTS
SHREDDED UNSWEETENED
COCONUT

PREPARATION | To make the meringue, pour the egg whites into the bowl of a stand mixer with the sugar and cornstarch. Whisk the egg whites at medium-high speed for about 8 minutes. The resulting meringue should be firm and glossy, so if necessary, increase the whisking time. Drizzle in the vinegar and whisk for 1 additional minute. Preheat the oven to 210°F (100°C) and line two baking sheets with parchment paper.

MAKE THE MERINGUE LADYFINGERS | Scoop the meringue mixture into a pastry bag fitted with a ⅜-inch (1-cm) tip (see page 17). Pipe out shapes as shown in the photo (see page 94), leaving an inch or more between them, as they expand while baking. Bake for 1 hour, until they are crisp outside, slightly soft inside, and easy to lift from the parchment paper. Let cool completely on the baking sheets.

MAKE THE COATING | Melt the chocolate (if you are using both dark and milk chocolate, melt them separately). Dip half of each ladyfinger into the melted chocolate and place on a baking sheet lined with parchment paper. If you wish, sprinkle with chopped nuts or shredded coconut. Place the baking sheet in the refrigerator until the chocolate sets, then remove and store in an airtight container.

OUR TIPS | If you want the chocolate to have a lovely sheen you can temper it beforehand. Chop two-thirds of the chocolate you have opted to use and set it to melt over a hot water bath. Meanwhile, finely chop the remaining one-third. When the melted chocolate is perfectly smooth, remove it from the heat and add the remaining chopped chocolate. Let it melt gently. When the mixture is smooth again, bring a little to your lips to test the temperature. It should be warm but not feel hot—you're aiming for a temperature of 88°F (31°C). If the chocolate firms up before you have finished coating the tips of the meringues, reheat it, ensuring that the temperature does not exceed 88°F (31°C).

VARIATIONS ON A THEME | Use other kinds of nuts to sprinkle on the chocolate—pecans and macadamias are a good choice. Go ahead and try chocolate shavings or even chopped candies. The possibilities are endless!

MERINGUE-KISS MACARONS

MAKES ABOUT 50 MACARONS

FOR THE GANACHE
¾ CUP (200 ML) WHIPPING CREAM

ZEST OF ½ LEMON, PREFERABLY ORGANIC

7 OZ. (200 G) DARK CHOCOLATE, CHOPPED

FOR THE MERINGUE
5 LARGE EGG WHITES (5 OZ /150 G), AT ROOM TEMPERATURE

1 CUP PLUS 1 TBSP. (7½ OZ./215 G) SUPERFINE SUGAR

1½ TBSP. (15 G) CORNSTARCH

1 TSP. WHITE WINE VINEGAR

7 OZ. (200 G) DARK CHOCOLATE, FOR DIPPING

PREPARATION | A day ahead, heat the cream for the ganache. Just before it comes to a boil, pour it over the lemon zest in a small bowl. Let cool slightly, cover with plastic wrap, and chill.

The next day, make the meringue: Preheat the oven to 210°F (100°C) and line two baking sheets with parchment paper. Pour the egg whites into the bowl of a stand mixer with the sugar and cornstarch. Whisk at medium-high speed for about 8 minutes. The resulting meringue should be firm and glossy, so if necessary, increase the whisking time. Drizzle in the vinegar and whisk for 1 additional minute.

Scoop the meringue mixture into a pastry bag fitted with a ⅜-inch (1-cm) plain tip (see page 17). Pipe out 1-inch (2.5-cm) diameter kisses, leaving an inch or more between them—they will expand while baking. Bake for 1 hour, until crisp outside, slightly soft inside, and easy to lift from the parchment paper. Let cool completely on the baking sheets.

ASSEMBLY | Melt the dark chocolate for dipping, then carefully dip the flat part of each meringue kiss into the chocolate and place on a baking sheet lined with parchment paper. Transfer to the refrigerator to let the chocolate set.

To finish the ganache, strain the lemon zest-infused cream, heat it to a simmer, and pour it over the chocolate in a round-bottomed mixing bowl. Wait 2 minutes, then make the ganache (see page 26). Let the ganache cool slightly, until it is firm enough to pipe, then transfer it to a pastry bag. Pipe a dollop of ganache onto the flat side of half of the meringue kisses, then assemble in pairs. Place in an airtight container and refrigerate until serving.

OUR TIPS | Meringue-kiss macarons are even better the following day.

VARIATIONS ON A THEME | You can sub milk chocolate for dark, and spice up the ganache with different flavorings, such as other citrus zests, spices, or tea.

FRENCH MARSHMALLOWS

By Gilles Marchal

MAKES ABOUT 25 MARSHMALLOWS

20 SHEETS (1½ OZ./40 G) GOLD-STRENGTH GELATIN

3⅔ CUPS (1½ LB./700 G) SUPERFINE SUGAR

SCANT ½ CUP (5 OZ./150 G) GLUCOSE SYRUP

1 CUP (250 ML) MINERAL WATER

4 LARGE EGG WHITES (4½ OZ./120 G), AT ROOM TEMPERATURE

SUGGESTED FLAVORINGS AND COLORINGS (SEE OUR TIPS)

2 TBSP. ORANGE BLOSSOM WATER

ZEST OF 2 ORANGES OR 3 LIMES, PREFERABLY ORGANIC

A SMALL AMOUNT OF YOUR FOOD COLORING OF CHOICE (POWDER OR GEL)

OR THE SEEDS OF 1 VANILLA BEAN

FOR DUSTING

1 GENEROUS CUP (5¼ OZ./150 G) CONFECTIONERS' SUGAR

¾ CUP (3½ OZ./100 G) POTATO STARCH

PREPARATION | A day ahead, soften the gelatin sheets in a bowl of cold water for about 15 minutes. Meanwhile, line a perfectly flat baking sheet with parchment paper or a silicone baking mat and top with a 6-inch (15-cm) square stainless steel confectionery frame at least 1¼ inches (3 cm) deep (or use a rigid baking pan). Squeeze excess water from the gelatin and melt in a saucepan over low heat or in a bowl in the microwave.

In a separate saucepan, begin heating the sugar, glucose, and water over medium heat. Pour the egg whites into the bowl of a stand mixer. When the sugar syrup reaches 250°F (120°C), begin whisking the whites at medium speed. When the sugar syrup reaches 260°F (128°C), carefully drizzle it down the side of the bowl into the egg whites with the mixer still running. Increase the speed and whisk in the warm melted gelatin.

Add your chosen flavoring and/or coloring and beat at high speed until firm.

Pour the warm marshmallow mixture into the confectionery frame. Let rest at room temperature for 24 hours.

The next day, sift the confectioners' sugar and potato starch together. Run a knife along the inside edge of the frame and remove it, then dust the surface of the marshmallow square with the sugar-starch mixture. Lay a sheet of parchment paper over the marshmallow square, turn it over, and remove the paper. Dust the second surface with the sugar-starch mixture. Using a long, thin knife, cut the marshmallow into 1-inch (3-cm) strips, then cut the strips into 1-inch (3-cm) cubes. Lightly toss in the remaining sugar-starch mixture to coat.

OUR TIPS | Flavor the marshmallows with various citrus zests or other seasonings like cinnamon, tonka beans, or pepper.

VARIATIONS ON A THEME | For your children's birthday parties, make marshmallow skewers, alternating the marshmallows with fresh fruit. Or dip the marshmallows in melted milk or dark chocolate and then roll them in finely chopped almonds or hazelnuts, or even rainbow sprinkles.

MERINGUE, REVISITED BY TOP GUEST PASTRY CHEFS

WALNUT VACHERIN

ALAIN FAUGÉROLAS,
PASTRY CHEF IN EXCIDEUIL, DORDOGNE

I SPENT MY CHILDHOOD VACATIONS IN THE DORDOGNE, IN
THE VERDANT REGION OF THE PÉRIGORD. IT'S AN AREA FULL OF HISTORY,
AND GASTRONOMY IS ANOTHER OF ITS HIGHLIGHTS. THE WALNUT VACHERIN
BY ALAIN FAUGÉROLAS IS A FOND MEMORY FROM MY CHILDHOOD, AND HIS
SUMPTUOUS VERSION WAS OUR WEDDING CAKE TOO. I HAVE TO CONFESS:
I OWE MY LOVE FOR MERINGUES TO THIS VERY DESSERT IN PARTICULAR AND,
NATURALLY, TO ITS CREATOR.

SERVES 10

FOR THE MERINGUE
7 OZ. (200 G) EGG WHITES,
FROM 6 TO 7 EGGS, AT ROOM
TEMPERATURE
2 CUPS (14 OZ./400 G) SUPERFINE
SUGAR
SEEDS OF 1 VANILLA BEAN

FOR THE ICE CREAM
2 CUPS (500 ML) WHOLE MILK

5 EGG YOLKS
⅔ CUP (4½ OZ./125 G) SUPERFINE
SUGAR
1 OZ. (25 G) INVERT SUGAR
(TRIMOLINE)
1 TSP. (5 ML) NATURAL VANILLA
EXTRACT, OR THE SEEDS OF
2 VANILLA BEANS
1 TBSP. (15 ML) WALNUT FLAVORING
3½ OZ. (100 G) CHOPPED WALNUTS,
ABOUT 1 SCANT CUP

FOR DECORATING
1¼ CUPS (300 ML) WHIPPING
CREAM, WELL CHILLED
3 TBSP. PLUS 1 TSP. (1½ OZ./40 G)
SUPERFINE SUGAR
SEEDS OF 1 VANILLA BEAN
2 HANDFULS LIGHTLY TOASTED
SLICED ALMONDS
ABOUT 15 WHOLE WALNUTS

A day ahead

MAKE THE MERINGUE | In a heatproof bowl, using a whisk or electric beater, whisk
the egg whites with the sugar to combine. Transfer to a hot water bath and continue
whisking until the mixture reaches a temperature of between 95°F (35°C) and 104°F
(40°C). Remove the bowl from the hot water bath, add the vanilla seeds, and continue
whisking for an additional 25 to 30 minutes.
Butter and flour a baking sheet and preheat the oven to 250°F (120°C).
With a pastry bag, pipe out three meringue disks of approximately 8 inches (20 cm)
in diameter and bake for 3½ hours.

MAKE THE ICE CREAM | Scald the milk. In the meantime, whisk the egg yolks with
the sugar and trimoline until the mixture is pale and thick. Gradually pour the hot milk
into the yolk mixture, whisking constantly. Return the preparation to low heat, stirring
nonstop, until the mixture coats the back of a spoon. Strain through a fine-mesh
sieve and incorporate the vanilla and walnut flavoring. Let cool slightly
and refrigerate until well chilled. Churn in an ice-cream maker according to the
manufacturer's instructions, then incorporate the chopped walnuts.

ASSEMBLE THE VACHERIN | Spread a layer of ice cream over a meringue disk and set a second disk neatly over the ice cream. Repeat the procedure once more and place in the freezer to firm up for at least 12 hours or overnight.

The next day

DECORATE THE VACHERIN | Whisk the cream with the sugar and vanilla seeds until it holds soft peaks. Spread the cream around the sides of the frozen vacherin and press with the sliced almonds. Using a pastry bag fitted with a star tip, pipe swirls of cream over the top of the vacherin and decorate with the walnuts.
Return to the freezer until 15 minutes before serving.

OUR TIPS | Trimoline, or inverted sugar syrup, prevents ice creams and sorbets from crystalizing. If you cannot find any, simply replace it with glucose syrup and carob flour to ensure that the ice cream has a lovely creamy texture when you take it out of the freezer.

Alain Faugérolas is a fourth-generation pastry chef who, with his wife Corinne, heads a family pastry shop that was founded by his great-grandfather in 1890 in the town of Excideuil. Their shop is renowned throughout the region for their pastries, cakes, and vacherins, many of which showcase the region's famous walnuts. Most popular of all is their generations-old recipe for the small walnut-shaped cakes called, quite simply, *Les Noix du Périgord*.

TROPICAL GUSTS

CHOCOLATE–COATED PASSION FRUIT WIND CRYSTALS FILLED WITH RASPBERRY JELLY

HERVÉ ROBIN, CHOCOLATE MAKER, PÉRIGEUX

I MET HERVÉ WHEN WE WERE BOTH WORKING AT LA MAISON DE CHOCOLAT, A PRODUCER OF DELUXE CHOCOLATE. I WAS IMMEDIATELY TAKEN WITH HIS GENEROSITY, HIS TALENT, AND LACK OF PRETENSE. AN ESTHETE WITH REFINED TASTES, HE FOUNDED HIS OWN WORKSHOP NEAR PÉRIGUEUX, THE CAPITAL OF THE PÉRIGORD REGION, AND HAS LAUNCHED HIS OWN COLLECTION OF EXCEPTIONAL CHOCOLATES. TO MY MIND, THEY ARE AMONG THE VERY FINEST ONE CAN FIND. FOR THIS BOOK, HE WAS KIND ENOUGH TO CREATE AN ORIGINAL RECIPE INCORPORATING ONE OF THE LATEST DEVELOPMENTS IN THE WORLD OF MERINGUES: *CRYSTAUX DE VENT* (WIND CRYSTALS), LIGHTER-THAN-AIR CONCOCTIONS INSPIRED BY THE RESEARCH OF TWO STANDARD-BEARERS OF MOLECULAR GASTRONOMY. WHAT'S MORE, WE ARE DELIGHTED THAT HE HAS ENTRUSTED US TO SELL HIS CHOCOLATE CREATIONS TO OUR CLIENTS.

SERVES 6

WIND CRYSTALS

THIS RECIPE WAS INSPIRED BY THE EXPERIMENTS CARRIED OUT BY MICHELIN-STARRED CHEF PIERRE GAGNAIRE IN COLLABORATION WITH CHEMIST HERVÉ THIS

.

FOR THE PASSION FRUIT WIND CRYSTALS

2 LARGE EGG WHITES (2 OZ./60G), AT ROOM TEMPERATURE

A DRIZZLE OF LEMON JUICE, AT ROOM TEMPERATURE

SCANT ⅓ CUP TO SCANT ½ CUP (60 TO 80 G) SUPERFINE SUGAR, TO TASTE

1 TBSP. PLUS 1 TSP. (20 ML) PASSION FRUIT JUICE, AT ROOM TEMPERATURE

SCANT ¼ CUP (1 OZ./30 G) CONFECTIONERS' SUGAR

FOR THE RASPBERRY JELLY

10 OZ. (300 G) RASPBERRIES

½ CUP (3½ OZ./100 G) LIGHT BROWN SUGAR

2 TSP. (8 G) AGAR AGAR

FOR THE COATING

1 LB. 2 OZ. (500 G) DARK CHOCOLATE (75% CACAO)

MAKE THE PASSION FRUIT WIND CRYSTALS | Preheat the oven to 250°F (120°C) and line a baking sheet with parchment paper.

Place the egg whites and lemon juice in a round-bottomed mixing bowl. With an electric mixer or the whisk of a stand mixer, lightly beat to combine. Increase the speed to medium and whisk until the whites hold firm peaks. Gradually add the superfine sugar and whisk at the same speed until the mixture is glossy. Drizzle in the passion fruit juice, whisking constantly. Stop when the juice is well incorporated. With a flexible spatula, fold in the confectioners' sugar. Using a pastry bag fitted with a ⅜-inch (1-cm) plain tip, pipe out the meringues onto the prepared baking sheet. Bake for 1 hour, until firm both outside and inside. Do not overbake!

MAKE THE RASPBERRY JELLY | In a saucepan (preferably copper) over low heat, gently cook the raspberries with the sugar until reduced. Process to blend and strain through a fine-mesh sieve into a separate small saucepan. Stir in the agar agar and bring to a boil, then remove from the heat, cover, and reserve at room temperature.

SCOOP OUT, FILL, AND COAT THE WIND CRYSTALS | When the crystals have cooled, use a ⅜-inch (1-cm) open star tip to scrape out the base and make a little hollow.

MAKE THE COATING | To temper the chocolate, roughly chop two-thirds and melt it in a heatproof bowl over a hot water bath, stirring regularly. Remove from the heat. Chop the remaining chocolate finely and stir it into the melted chocolate to melt gently. When the chocolate is smooth, test it by touching it to your lips: it should be lukewarm, not hot. The ideal temperature is 88°F (31°C) but this may vary by a degree or two depending on the chocolate you use. Without any further ado, coat the wind crystals with the tempered chocolate, setting aside a little to seal the holes you will be making, and place them on a rack with a rimmed pan below to allow the excess chocolate to drip off.

When the chocolate coating has set, spoon the raspberry jelly into a pastry bag. Make a small hole at the base of each confection and pipe in a small amount of the jelly. Use a flexible spatula to seal the opening with the remaining tempered chocolate. If it has started to set, reheat it quickly, ensuring the temperature does not exceed 88°F (31°C).

Serve immediately, because they become moist quickly and do not stay crisp for long.

OUR TIPS | Any preparation made with agar agar can be liquidized again. If the raspberry jelly sets before you manage to fill the wind crystals, there's no need to panic. Simply reheat it to about 77°F (25°C). And ensure that the passion fruit juice is at the same temperature as the egg whites, and no warmer!

VARIATIONS ON A THEME | The possibilities are endless. In summer, why not make mint-flavored wind crystals? Infuse chopped mint leaves in cold water about 12 hours ahead and use the liquid, at room temperature, instead of the juice. For the filling, lime jelly with a dash of rum is divine.

PRALINE ZEPHYRS
COFFEE-FLAVORED WIND CRYSTALS FILLED WITH HAZELNUT PRALINE

SERVES 6

FOR THE COFFEE-FLAVORED WIND CRYSTALS

2 LARGE EGG WHITES (2 OZ./60 G), AT ROOM TEMPERATURE

A DRIZZLE OF LEMON JUICE, AT ROOM TEMPERATURE

SCANT ⅓ CUP TO SCANT ½ CUP (60 TO 80 G) SUGAR, TO TASTE

1 TBSP. PLUS 1 TSP. (20 ML) BLACK COFFEE, COOLED TO ROOM TEMPERATURE

SCANT ¼ CUP (1 OZ./30 G) CONFECTIONERS' SUGAR

FOR THE HAZELNUT PRALINE

2 TBSP. (15 G) POWDERED MILK

SCANT ⅓ CUP (2 OZ./60 G) LIGHT BROWN SUGAR

SCANT ⅓ CUP (2 OZ./60 G) GRANULATED SUGAR

6 OZ. (180 G) SKINNED HAZELNUTS (ABOUT 1⅓ CUPS)

2 OZ. (50 G) MILK CHOCOLATE, CHOPPED

2 OZ. (50 G) CACAO BUTTER, CHOPPED

FOR THE COATING

1 LB. 2 OZ. (500 G) DARK CHOCOLATE (75% CACAO)

MAKE THE WIND CRYSTALS | Follow the procedure on page 106, replacing the passion fruit juice with the black coffee. Do ensure that the egg whites and coffee are both at room temperature.

MAKE THE HAZELNUT PRALINE | Preheat the oven to 340°F (170°C). Toast the powdered milk, stirring it regularly, until golden. Reduce the oven temperature to 265°F (130°C).

To make the syrup, pour the two types of sugar into a saucepan, preferably copper, and add 3 tablespoons (40 ml) of water. Place on medium-high heat. Spread the hazelnuts across a baking sheet and toast for about 10 minutes; do not allow to burn. The nuts must remain warm for the next step.

When the syrup reaches 243°F (117°C), add the hazelnuts, stirring constantly (see Our tips). Continue stirring until the sugar reaches a grainy texture and slowly starts to coat the hazelnuts with caramel. If the mixture seems to be caramelizing too fast, reduce the heat. Caramel must have a pronounced color to be flavorful, so do not remove it from the heat while it is still too light. Spread the caramelized hazelnuts on a sheet of non-stick paper and let cool.

In a food processor, place the powdered milk and caramelized hazelnuts and blend very roughly. Transfer to an airtight container and freeze for 1 hour.

Return the mixture to the food processor and process until it reaches the consistency you prefer for your praline. While you are processing, check that the temperature does not exceed 84°F (29°C) or it might separate. The final texture can be very thick, somewhat thick, runny—it's your choice.

SCOOP OUT AND COAT THE WIND CRYSTALS | Following the procedure in the recipe above (page 106), temper the dark chocolate, then scoop out the base of the wind crystals and coat them with the tempered chocolate. Finish the praline and fill the wind crystals: melt the milk chocolate over a hot water bath. Remove from the heat and add the cacao butter, which should melt slowly. Stir until just smooth and check the temperature, which should be around 88°F (31°C). If the mixture is too hot, stir in a little more chopped milk chocolate. When smooth, incorporate the praline, spoon it into a pastry bag, and fill the hollows. Following the instructions on page 106, seal the base of each one with tempered chocolate left over from the coating.

OUR TIPS | Should you inadvertently allow the temperature of the syrup to exceed 243°F (117°C), simply add a little water and wait until the syrup reaches the correct temperature. To check the caramel for doneness, scoop a little from the saucepan with a piece of baking paper. It's all a question of color: too pale and it will have no taste, so ideally you should cook it to a dark brown color. It takes a careful eye!

VARIATIONS ON A THEME | Of course, you can use this recipe to make praline with almonds, pecans, and walnuts too.

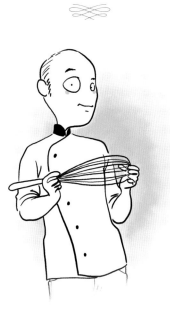

Hervé Robin honed his trade with renowned chef Christian Constant, at the long-established Parisian pastry shop Dalloyau, and at Oberweis, a Luxembourg–based food emporium. For over twenty years now, Hervé has been sharing his love for chocolate with his lucky clients, who enjoy the subtle pairings of his ganaches and his delectable praline creations. He founded his own chocolate shop in the town of Périgueux in 2013.

TOUSLED LIME MERINGUE TART

GILLES MARCHAL, PASTRY CHEF, PARIS

I FIRST ENCOUNTERED GILLES MARCHAL'S "TOUSLED" LIME MERINGUE TART
WHEN HE WAS STILL AT LE BRISTOL, BEFORE I'D MET HIM IN PERSON. IT BLEW
ME AWAY. WE LATER WORKED TOGETHER AT LA MAISON DU CHOCOLAT.
GILLES HAS AN INCREDIBLY CREATIVE APPROACH TO PASTRY-MAKING,
YET HIS CREATIONS REMAIN UNPRETENTIOUS AND DELICIOUS.
HIS LIME MERINGUE TART IS SIMPLY DIVINE.

SERVES 6

FOR THE LIGHTLY CANDIED LIME SECTIONS

3 LIMES, PREFERABLY ORGANIC

SCANT ½ CUP (100 ML) MINERAL WATER

2½ TSP. (10 G) SUGAR

FOR THE MERINGUE

3 LARGE EGG WHITES (3 OZ./90 G), AT ROOM TEMPERATURE

SCANT ½ CUP (3 OZ./80 G) SUPERFINE SUGAR

2 PINCHES FINE SEA SALT

GRATED ZEST OF 1 LIME (FROM ABOVE)

1 VERY SMALL PINCH OF GREEN FOOD COLORING, GEL OR POWDER

⅔ CUP (3 OZ./80 G) CONFECTIONERS' SUGAR, SIFTED

FOR THE LIME CREAM

1 SHEET GELATIN

2 SMALL EGGS (3 OZ./90 G)

SCANT ½ CUP (3 OZ./80 G) SUPERFINE SUGAR

ZEST OF 3 LIMES, PREFERABLY ORGANIC

JUICE OF 2 LIMES, STRAINED

7 TBSP. (4 OZ./110 G) UNSALTED BUTTER, WELL CHILLED AND DICED

FOR THE SWEET SHORTCRUST PASTRY

6 TBSP. (3 OZ./90 G) EUROPEAN-STYLE BUTTER, WELL CHILLED AND DICED, PLUS MORE FOR THE PAN

SCANT ½ CUP (2 OZ. / 60 G) CONFECTIONERS' SUGAR, SIFTED

3 TBSP. (15 G) GROUND ALMONDS

1 SMALL EGG (1½ OZ./40 G)

1⅓ CUPS (5½ OZ./160 G) FLOUR, SIFTED

2 PINCHES FINE SEA SALT

FOR DECORATING

ZEST OF 1 OR 2 LIMES, PREFERABLY ORGANIC

A day ahead

MAKE THE LIGHTLY CANDIED LIME SECTIONS | Grate the zest of one of the limes and
reserve for the meringue. Using a sharp knife, peel and segment all of the limes (see
page 22).

In a saucepan, heat the water and sugar to boiling, then carefully pour the hot syrup
over the lime sections in a bowl to candy them lightly. Let cool, cover, and refrigerate
for 12 hours or overnight.

MAKE THE MERINGUE | Preheat the oven to 210°F (100°C) and line two baking sheets with parchment paper or silicone baking mats. Fit a pastry bag with a ¼-inch (6-mm) plain tip.

Using an electric mixer or whisk, beat the egg whites with half of the superfine sugar and the salt until they are smooth and hold firm peaks. Beating gently, sprinkle in the remaining superfine sugar, then incorporate the lime zest and green food coloring (take care—you need very little for a lovely pastel green). Using a flexible spatula, gently fold in the confectioners' sugar.

Scoop the meringue mixture into the pastry bag and pipe out long, thin cylinders lengthwise on the baking sheets—be sure to space the cylinders about ¼ inch (5 mm) apart.

Bake for 1 hour to 1 hour 20 minutes, until the meringue is thoroughly dry. As soon as you remove the meringue from the oven, cut it into 2½ to 3-inch (6 to 8-cm) pieces with a knife.

Let the meringue cool completely on the baking sheets, then carefully transfer it to an airtight container and store in a cool, dry place.

MAKE THE LIME CREAM | Soften the gelatin sheet in a bowl of cold water.

In a saucepan, combine the eggs, sugar, and lime zest and juice. Slowly heat to boiling over low heat, stirring constantly with a whisk. Immediately remove from the heat, stir in the butter, then return to a simmer and cook for 1 additional minute, still whisking nonstop.

Strain the cream mixture through a fine-mesh strainer. Gently squeeze the excess water from the gelatin sheet and stir it into the warm cream until completely dissolved. Let cool, cover, and refrigerate for at least 3 hours.

TO MAKE THE SWEET SHORTCRUST PASTRY | In a mixing bowl, work the butter with a flexible spatula or the paddle attachment of a stand mixer until it is smooth and creamy. Incorporate the confectioners' sugar, ground almonds, egg, flour, and salt. Once the dough is smooth, shape it into a ball, then roll it out between two sheets of parchment paper into an 8-inch (20-cm) circle that is just over ⅛ inch (4 to 5 mm) thick. Refrigerate for 2 hours.

Lightly butter a tart pan or a stainless steel tart circle. Line the pan with the dough and refrigerate for 2 additional hours.

Preheat the oven to between 300°F (150°C) and 320°F (160°C), then bake the crust for about 30 minutes, until the top and bottom are uniformly golden. Let cool completely and store in an airtight container in a cool, dry place.

ASSEMBLY: One hour before serving (so that the meringue remains as crisp as possible), drain the candied lime sections and arrange them over the crust. Pour the lime cream over the lime sections and carefully spread it out into an even layer using an offset spatula. Sprinkle with the zest of 1 to 1½ limes. Carefully stand the meringue pieces up in the cream to make an attractive, whimsical design, akin to tousled hair. Decorate with the zest of ½ lime.

OUR TIPS: Use lemon or yuzu in place of the lime in the same proportions. Or swap out the lightly candied lime sections for lemon or orange marmalade, homemade raspberry jam with seeds, or fresh strawberries or raspberries.

Gilles Marchal has fond memories of his childhood in Laneuveville-aux-Bois, his native village in Lorraine; of his grandmother, who always cooked with farm-fresh ingredients; and of his father, who sold chocolates, which Gilles would melt down with his mother to make his first sweet creations. At the age of fourteen, he began apprenticing with Claude Bourguignon, an iconic pastry chef in Lorraine, and he later donned the pastry sous-chef apron at the Hôtel de Crillon in Paris. He then worked as head pastry chef at two other prestigious Paris hotels—the Plaza Athénée and Le Bristol—before becoming creative director at La Maison du Chocolat, also in the City of Light. In 2004, a prestigious pastry magazine named him pastry chef of the year in Paris, and in 2008, the city awarded him a medal for his services to pastry-making in France. In 2014, he opened his own pastry shop in the French capital, at 9 rue Ravignan in the Montmartre neighborhood. This enchanting, village like corner of Paris—where people take the time to enjoy life and to get to know one another—continues to inspire Gilles to do his most creative work.

TUTTI-FRUTTI

FABIEN ROUILLARD, PASTRY CHEF AND OWNER, MAISON MULOT, PARIS

I MET FABIEN IN ANOTHER RENOWNED GOURMET DESTINATION IN PARIS— FAUCHON. AS PASTRY CHEF AT THIS FABULOUS FOOD EMPORIUM, FABIEN CONVEYED HIS PERSONALITY IN HIS CREATIONS, COMBINING RIGOR AND PERFECTION WITH REMARKABLE CREATIVITY. WITH HIS CHARACTERISTIC HUMILITY, HE IS A STICKLER FOR INGREDIENTS THAT ARE OF THE HIGHEST QUALITY. HE HAS GENEROUSLY SHARED THIS RECIPE FOR TUTTI-FRUTTI MERINGUE—ONE OF HIS ALL-TIME CLASSICS—WITH US. THANK YOU, FABIEN!

SERVES 6

2 LB. (1 KG) ASSORTED DICED
CANDIED FRUIT

15 TO 16 LARGE EGG WHITES
(1 LB./500 G), AT ROOM
TEMPERATURE

4 CUPS (1¾ LB./800 G) SUGAR

1 PINCH SALT

CONFECTIONERS' SUGAR,
FOR DUSTING

VANILLA ICE CREAM TO SERVE 6

ABOUT 10 AMARENA CHERRIES IN
SYRUP

PREPARATION | Preheat the oven to 200°F (90°C) and line a baking sheet with parchment paper. Set on a second baking sheet to prevent burning. Put the candied fruit in a colander so that any excess liquid can drain, and place six plates in the freezer at least 2 hours before serving.

Pour the egg whites into the bowl of a stand mixer with half of the sugar and the salt. Whisk at medium speed for 4 minutes, then gradually add the remaining sugar, whisking nonstop. Increase the speed to high and beat until the meringue holds firm, glossy peaks. Using a flexible spatula, gently fold in the candied fruit.

Using a slotted skimmer dipped in ice-cold water, scoop up about one-sixth of the meringue and set it on the prepared baking sheet. Let the meringue spread out on its own to obtain a lovely free-form shape. Repeat five times, dipping the skimmer in cold water each time.

Bake for 1 hour and dust immediately with confectioners' sugar. Let cool completely on the baking sheet.

Pick up each meringue and gently tap the bottom to break the outer shell. Fill generously with vanilla ice cream and set on the plates from the freezer. Decorate with the Amarena cherries and drizzle with the cherry syrup.

Pick up a spoon, close your eyes, bite in, and rejoice!

Fabien Rouillard has worn many hats (chef, pastry chef, consultant, and even that of a UN peacekeeper in Somalia), but it is that of artisan that best suits his creative and entrepreneurial spirit. Fabien graduated from the prestigious Vatel Institute in 1992 and in 1998 was hired as pastry chef at the starred Lucas Carton restaurant in Paris, joining chef Alain Senderens. In 2001, driven by a taste for innovation, he co-founded the Créations Conseil Desserts agency. After a stint at the Sketch restaurant in London, Fabien took over from Christophe Adam at Fauchon in 2011, where he became the creative director. He held this position until 2015, when he met the legendary pastry chef Gérard Mulot, who was looking for a successor. Today, Fabien is at the helm of the eponymous Parisian pastry institution Mulot founded.

MARCO POLO

GAËL CLAVIÈRE, HEAD PASTRY CHEF
AT THE HÔTEL DE MATIGNON

GAËL AND I MET AS CHOCOLATE AFICIONADOS AT A MEETING OF THE CLUB
DE CROQUEURS DE CHOCOLAT. BETWEEN CHOCOLATE TASTINGS, WE TALKED
PASTRY. GAËL'S ENTHUSIASM AND FRIENDLINESS ARE CONTAGIOUS,
AND BOTH COME ACROSS IN HIS RECIPES. HIS TALENT SHINES THROUGH
IN THIS EXQUISITE CREATION THAT MIGHT WELL BE ENJOYED BY THE FRENCH
PRIME MINISTER AND HIS DISTINGUISHED GUESTS.

SERVES 10

FOR THE STAR ANISE-INFUSED CARAMEL CREAM
1 CUP PLUS 3 TBSP. (280 ML) WHOLE MILK
1⅜ CUPS (330 ML) WHIPPING CREAM TO HEAT
2 STAR ANISE PODS
1 SHEET (2 G) GOLD-STRENGTH GELATIN
⅔ CUP (4½ OZ./125 G) SUPERFINE SUGAR
3 LARGE EGG YOLKS (2 OZ./55 G)
3 TBSP. (1 OZ./30 G) FLOUR

7¾ OZ. (220 G) BLOND DULCEY CHOCOLATE, CHOPPED
3⅓ CUPS (800 ML) HEAVY WHIPPING CREAM, WELL CHILLED

FOR THE MERINGUE BASES
8 LARGE EGG WHITES (9 OZ./250 G), AT ROOM TEMPERATURE
1¼ CUPS (9 OZ./250 G) SUPERFINE SUGAR
1 TSP. (5 ML) LEMON JUICE
A HEAPING ¼ TSP. (1 G) CREAM OF TARTAR

2 CUPS (9 OZ./250 G) CONFECTIONERS' SUGAR, SIFTED

FOR THE PINK RHUBARB COMPOTE
7 OZ. (200 G) PINK RHUBARB
1 TBSP. PLUS 2 TSP. (20 G) SUGAR
A LITTLE ORGANIC LIME ZEST (OPTIONAL)

FOR THE TOPPING
1 STALK RHUBARB
4 OZ. (125 G) STRAWBERRIES

MAKE THE STAR ANISE-INFUSED CARAMEL CREAM | A day ahead, combine the milk, whipping cream, and star anise pods in a bowl. Cover and chill.
The next day, soften the gelatin in a bowl of cold water and begin heating the infused cream in a saucepan. In a separate saucepan, caramelize a scant ½ cup (85 g) of the sugar over low heat until dark golden brown. Remove the star anise pods from the hot cream and carefully whisk the cream into the caramel to deglaze it. Remove from the heat.
Whisk the egg yolks with the remaining sugar until pale and thick. Whisk in the flour, then gradually add the caramel cream. Transfer to a saucepan and cook over low heat, stirring, until thickened. Wring the gelatin dry and place in a large bowl with the chocolate. Stir in the hot caramel cream and let cool to 86°F (30°C).
Whisk the heavy whipping cream to firm peaks, then fold in the caramel-chocolate mixture.

MAKE THE MERINGUE BASES | Preheat the oven to 175°F (80°C) in convection mode. Line two baking sheets with parchment paper and cut out two 2¾-inch (7-cm) parchment paper circles for each serving. Fit a pastry bag with a ¼-inch (7-mm) plain tip.
Using a stand mixer, whisk the egg whites with ¼ cup (2 oz./50 g) of the superfine sugar, the lemon juice, and the cream of tartar at medium-high speed until soft peaks form, incorporating 2 tablespoons (25 g) of superfine sugar after 3 minutes. Add the remaining superfine sugar and beat at high speed for 5 minutes, until the whites hold firm peaks. With a slotted skimmer, fold in the confectioners' sugar. Use the pastry bag to pipe out a meringue spiral onto each parchment circle, then pipe teardrop shapes around both. Fit a ¾-inch (2-mm) plain tip on a second pastry bag and pipe out thin cylinders onto the baking sheet alongside the spirals. Bake for about 1½ hours, until crisp. Let cool completely on the baking sheet(s).

MAKE THE PINK RHUBARB COMPOTE | Peel the rhubarb and remove the stringy fibers. Cut the fruit into pieces, toss with the sugar in a bowl, and let sit for several hours to release its juice. Finely dice half of the rhubarb and cook the remaining half with the sugar and juice until the fruit has broken down and the mixture has thickened. Let cool completely, then combine with the diced rhubarb. If you like, add a little lime zest for a refreshing note.

MAKE THE TOPPING | To make the rhubarb chips, preheat the oven to 160°F (70°C). Using a vegetable peeler, remove paper-thin slices of rhubarb and blanch them in boiling water with a little sugar. Drain and bake for 30 minutes, turning occasionally, until dry. Wash, hull, and quarter the strawberries.

ASSEMBLY | Place one of the meringue bases on a serving plate. Using a pastry bag fitted with a ¼-inch (7-mm) plain tip, pipe out small mounds of the star anise-infused caramel-chocolate cream around the inner edge of the teardrop border. Place a little of the rhubarb compote in the center, then top with the second meringue base. Pipe out the cream around the teardrop border as above and place another dollop of the rhubarb compote in the center. Arrange the strawberries and rhubarb chips on top and decorate with the meringue cylinders. Repeat for each serving.

The word "eclectic" perfectly describes **Gaël Clavière**, a pastry chef who loves flying planes as much as horseback riding. Gaël first immersed himself in the pastry trade as an apprentice at two bakeries in the South of France—Donati and Marcot—where he fine-tuned his palate. Between 1996 and 2006, the apprentice perfected his skills at Fauchon, La Maison du Chocolat, and the prestigious catering firm Potel & Chabot, learning rigor and the importance of putting flavor first. Since 2006, he has practiced his exquisite, flavor-driven art as head pastry chef at the Hôtel de Matignon, the official residence of the French Prime Minister.

MERINGAIE PIE COCKTAIL

VIVIEN DADOUCHE FOR MONSIEUR VIVIEN

VIVIEN IS NOTHING LESS THAN A COCKTAIL ARTIST, AND I CAN GUARANTEE THAT YOU'VE NEVER TASTED CREATIONS AS GOOD AS HIS. HIS DISCOVERY OF OUR MERINGUES TRIGGERED A HANKERING TO MAKE AN ASTOUNDING COCKTAIL, AND YOU HAVE THE RESULTS HERE: A MINI-MERINGUE BROUGHT TO SUBLIME HEIGHTS IN A DRINK WITH AN INTRIGUING BLEND OF SUBTLE FLAVORS. DRINK IN MODERATION!

SERVES 1

FOR THE WINTER COCKTAIL
INFUSE 2½ OZ. (75 G) OF CRUSHED SPECULAAS COOKIES IN 1 BOTTLE ABSOLUT ELYX VODKA FOR 72 HOURS, THEN STRAIN THROUGH A FINE-MESH SIEVE THREE TIMES, UNTIL AS CLEAR AS POSSIBLE.

FOR THE SUMMER COCKTAIL
RINSE 3 STALKS OF LEMON GRASS, LEAVING THEM UNPEELED, AND CAREFULLY CUT EACH ONE INTO 4 LENGTHWISE. PLACE THEM IN THE BOTTLE OF VODKA FOR 72 HOURS.

WINTER MERINGAIE COCKTAIL PIE
2 TBSP. PLUS 2 TSP. (40 ML) SPECULAAS-INFUSED ABSOLUT ELYX VODKA

1 SPRIG FRESH TARRAGON

1 OZ. (30 G) FAT-FREE PLAIN ARTISANAL FROZEN YOGHURT

2 TSP. (10 ML) AMARETTO

2 TSP. (10 ML) MIXED LEMON AND LIME JUICE

3 TBSP. PLUS 1 TSP. (50 ML) SPARKLING LEMONADE

6 MERINGUETTES, PIPED WITH POINTED TIPS

ZEST OF 1 LIME, PREFERABLY ORGANIC

SUMMER MERINGAIE COCKTAIL PIE
2 TBSP. PLUS 2 TSP. (40 ML) LEMONGRASS-INFUSED ABSOLUT ELYX VODKA

3 LEAVES BASIL

1 OZ. (30 G) FAT-FREE PLAIN ARTISANAL FROZEN YOGHURT

½ PASSION FRUIT

4 RASPBERRIES

1 TBSP. (15 ML) LIME JUICE

3 TBSP. PLUS 1 TSP. (50 ML) SPARKLING LEMONADE

6 MERINGUETTES, PIPED WITH POINTED TIPS

ZEST OF 1 LIME, PREFERABLY ORGANIC

EDIBLE FOOD COLOR SPRAY (OPTIONAL)

PREPARATION | Depending on the version you are making, place the vodka and tarragon or basil leaves in a shaker without adding any ice cubes. Use a pestle to press on the herbs to bring out their essential oils. Add the frozen yoghurt and the remaining ingredients, with the exception of the sparkling lemonade, meringuettes, and lime zest.

Shake vigorously for 10 seconds. Pour the mixture into a Martini® glass. Pour in the sparkling lemonade, stopping just short of ¾ inch (2 cm) from the rim.
Spray the meringuettes with the food coloring, if using, and float them on the top of the drink, placing one in the center and the five others around it. Zest the lime over the meringuettes and pop a straw into the glass. *Chin-chin*!

OUR TIPS | To adapt the cocktail to your theme and to add a little color to this immaculately white drink, we recommend spraying a little natural food color on the meringuettes. Here, I've used a copper color. A word from the wise to enjoy the drink to the utmost: grab a meringuette by its tip, dunk it into the drink, and pop it into your mouth as you sip the liquid through the straw. The effect on the palate will be that of a lemon meringue pie.

An artist with diverse talents, self-taught **Vivien Dadouche**, a lover of fine dining and tableware, started his career in the fashion industry. This inspired him to adapt the codes and creativity of fashion to cocktails, updating them so they are more delicious and sexier all round. Vivien puts them together like a fashion collection: From the initial sketches to the flavor structure and the final showcase, the drinks—like models on a catwalk—are thought out to the last detail. Even the tiniest element counts towards the whole, just like in pastry-making. A decidedly innovative vision of the art of French cocktails!

ESPRESSO MERINGUE FLOAT

ARAKU COFFEE, EXCEPTIONAL COFFEE GROWN BIODYNAMICALLY IN THE ARAKU VALLEY IN INDIA

THIS ORIGINAL, CONTRASTING COMBINATION—HALFWAY BETWEEN COFFEE AND DESSERT—LOOKS LIKE A VIENNESE COFFEE AND SEEMS ALMOST TOO GORGEOUS TO TOUCH. BUT CATCH THE TIP OF THE MERINGUE BETWEEN YOUR FINGERS AFTER IT HAS SOAKED UP A LITTLE ESPRESSO, AND FIND THE MAGIC: BOLD COFFEE FLAVOR, SWEET MERINGUE, A CRISP SHELL—YUM!

FOR THE MERINGUE

5 LARGE EGG WHITES (5 OZ./150 G), AT ROOM TEMPERATURE

1 CUP PLUS 1 TBSP. (7½ OZ./215 G) SUPERFINE SUGAR

1½ TBSP. (15 G) CORNSTARCH

1 TSP. WHITE WINE VINEGAR

FOR THE ESPRESSO

ARAKU SELECTION, ARAKU SIGNATURE, OR YOUR FAVORITE ESPRESSO COFFEE (SEE OUR TIPS)

MAKE THE MERINGUE | Pour the egg whites into the bowl of a stand mixer with the sugar and cornstarch. Beat at medium-high speed for 10 minutes. The resulting meringue should be firm with glossy peaks, so increase the whisking time if necessary. Drizzle in the vinegar and whisk for 1 additional minute.

Preheat the oven to 210°F (100°C) and line a baking sheet with parchment paper. Scoop the meringue into a pastry bag fitted with a ⅜-inch plain tip (see page 17). Pipe out small meringue kisses onto the prepared baking sheet about 1 inch (2.5 cm) apart, as they expand while baking. Bake for 1 hour, until crisp outside and slightly soft inside. Let cool completely on the baking sheet.

ASSEMBLY | For each serving, prepare a cup of espresso with a nice layer of crema and gently float a meringue on top.

OUR TIPS | Coffee produced in the Araku Valley in India, sweet yet bold, is the perfect foil to the meringue in this recipe.

For a truly special treat, try the perfectly balanced Araku Signature with notes of chocolate and spice, or go for Araku Selection, which is richer and stronger with butter and spice flavors and a touch of bitterness that gives a greater contrast with the sweet meringue. Feel free to experiment by adding a pinch of vanilla, cinnamon, cardamom, or another spice to your favorite espresso coffees to find the combination you like best.

Photo on following page

LIST OF RECIPES

INDEX OF INGREDIENTS

ACKNOWLEDGMENTS

We would like to thank:

• Rina, an outstanding photographer who has shown our Meringaie pavlovas to their best advantage.

• Sarah, who has read our minds, using her talent and creativity to showcase the images we had envisaged.

• Marie, our editor, who directed, organized, and supported us cheerfully from the very outset of this exciting project.

• Emma, for her sketching talent. With just a few playful yet kind strokes of her pencil, she has captured the essence of each one of us.

• Florence, our graphic artist, who has achieved just the right balance—chic yet lighthearted—to display our Meringaies.

• Each member of the teams at Éditions de la Martinière, whose crazy idea it was to approach us about a book dedicated to meringues and pavlovas.

• Gilles Marchal, our friend, a big brother to us, a fine pastry-making artist, who reintroduced us to a taste for simple things accomplished to perfection.

• Alain Faugérolas, the pastry chef of my childhood. I owe my love of meringues to his creations, and in particular, to his now-famous walnut vacherin.

• Fabien Rouillard, a man who loves a challenge, who helped our project to see the light of day. We are grateful for his friendship, his modesty, and his talent.

• Hervé Robin, the chocolatier closest to our hearts. His creativity and talent are equaled only by his kindness.

• Gaël Clavière, pastry chef to the French Prime Minister who expertly wields his whisk in the halls of power, for his perpetual good cheer and his readiness to take up the wildest of challenges.

• Vivien Dadouche and his cocktails, which knock our socks off. We are so glad that he pushed open our door one day.

• All the team members at La Meringaie, for their exuberance and their enthusiasm for our creations. They make each day better for us.

• Olivier Desdoigts, for the talent he deployed in creating La Meringaie's visual identity.

• Caroline, our press attaché, for her commitment to developing and publicizing our desserts.

• All of our friends, who have helped and encouraged us from the very outset of this crazy enterprise.

• Our sons, Paul, Ernest, and Gabriel. They took La Meringaie in like a little sister, and all devote considerable time to the undertaking.

• My partner and husband, Benoît, who, one day, while eating one of the first pavlovas I had made, said, "It's just too good not to share." He was right. He took things in hand and today directs the business. Without him, none of this would have been possible.

• Finally, heartfelt thanks to Charlotte Sindou-Faurie, for her exquisite talents and subtle combinations of fruit and cream flavors, and for her unfailing commitment and affection.

OUR ADDRESSES

Pâtisserie Alain Faugérolas
1 avenue Gambetta, 24160 Excideuil • +33 (0)5 53 62 42 33

Pâtisserie Gilles Marchal
9 rue Ravignan, 75018 Paris • +33 (0)1 85 34 73 30
www.gillesmarchal.com

Fabien Rouillard, Maison Mulot
76 rue de Seine, 75006 Paris • +33 (0)1 43 26 85 77
www.gerard-mulot.com

Hervé Robin Chocolatier
1 avenue du 19-mars-1962, 24660 Notre-Dame-de-Sanilhac
+33 (0)5 53 45 78 34

Monsieur Vivien
6 rue de Naples, 75008 Paris • +33 (0)1 81 69 68 41
www.monsieurvivien.com

Araku Coffee
14 rue de Bretagne, 75003 Paris
online boutique : www.arakucoffee.com